DARE
TO LIVE

Jean-Marie Cardinal
Lustiger

DARE
TO LIVE

═══════════╤═══════════
＊

Translated by M. N. L. Couve de Murville

CROSSROAD · NEW YORK

1988

The Crossroad Publishing Company
370 Lexington Avenue, New York, N.Y. 10017

Originally published as *Osez vivre: Articles, conférences, sermons, interviews, 1981–1984, II*
© Editions du Centurion, 1985

Printed in the United States of America

Library of Congress Cataloging-in-Publication Data

Lustiger, Jean-Marie, 1926–
 [Osez vivre. English]
 Dare to live / Jean-Marie Cardinal Lustiger ; translated by M.N.L. Couve de Murville.

 p. cm.
 Translation of: Osez vivre.
 ISBN 0-8245-0873-4
 1. Catholic Church—Doctrines. 2. Catholic Church—History—1965–
I. Title.
BX1751.2.L8713 1988   88-3643
                                                                       CIP

Contents

YOUTH AND SCHOOL

CHURCH AND STATE

PEACE AND RECONCILIATION

Preface

I have just gone over the pages which you perhaps are now going to read, and I was surprised. All of this was originally said or written in French, and the thoughts are familiar to me. Yet at certain times it sounded to me as though it were new. And I wondered: Did I really say or write this or that? But I had to face the fact that the translation is perfect. It is due to an old and dear friend of mine, Archbishop Maurice Couve de Murville of Birmingham, England, who is also an outstanding scholar in his own right.

A curious experience indeed! The Italians say that to translate is to betray *(traduttore, traditore)*. In this case I would rather say that to translate is to disclose: the transfer from one language into another exposes human speech to unforeseen illuminations and may enhance it unexpectedly, just as changing light may make a landscape look different. The English language makes all these words sound new, although they were uttered or printed in French a few years ago. This is why I rather regret insisting on their being meticulously dated. Marketing specialists will probably think it foolish, believing that one should never confess how long ago something was produced, unless it is hidden away in small type at the back of the book. English-speaking readers, like their French counterparts, might spontaneously feel that what is a little old is bound to have lost its relevance and interest. But I rather agree with those who enjoy good wines: as they age, some wines improve their flavor and aroma; others become insipid. Time is a fearsome trial and you will be the jury.

Some of these pages, I am afraid, may taste and smell intolerably of "old Europe," because of their somewhat abstract turn. I am not sure whether an English-speaking audience is prepared to accord texts of this type the esteem that is due their author. Still and all, I invite you to stick to it. You will thus inhale a bit of the Parisian air and spirit, which consists in talking about everything, especially that which one does not understand, but with such brilliance that one gives the illusion of knowing all.

Please forgive my trying to be witty. The most important message of this book still consumes me: "Dare to live!" For life is God's gift to us. And more than ever it is threatened by our greatest enemy: ourselves. Humans are the only living things that must learn how to live. Our life is not merely a biological process. It is also a spiritual reality which nourishes itself with its freedom. The wish to live has to be learned and sustained. To want to live means to learn about life and *who* life is. The disciples of Jesus remember his words: "I am the way, and the truth, and the life" (John 14:6).

JEAN-MARIE CARDINAL LUSTIGER

Paris
Easter 1988

CHRISTIANITY HAS A FUTURE

———✳———

While History Unfolds

In times past, it was considered normal for human beings to die of hunger. *Famine*, like plague and war, seemed to be one of those scourges which were an unavoidable part of human destiny. Today the West no longer dies of hunger because it has succeeded in mastering nature; it has done so by its will to work, by its potential in mobilizing resources, and by its scientific and technical advances. The West owes this success to Christianity, whether it knows it or not. It is the Word of God which has revealed to it that the universe proceeds from God's creative goodness toward human life. It is God's Word which has given it the hope of being filled with good things and it is God's Word which has given it the duty of sharing one's bread with those who have none.

The West no longer starves but there is still starvation in the world. The reasons for famine, however, can no longer be laid at the door of nature or of fate, as if it were a calamity which humankind cannot overcome, because now it is our determination to possess the world which gives rise to hunger in the world. It is basically in the human heart that the causes of hunger in the world now reside. The Christian faith has given rise to hope; famine is not unavoidable. But this hope will be disappointed if men and women are not converted, and the disappointment will be bitter indeed because that hope is capable of fulfillment and everybody knows it.

People used to think that *violence* constituted a basic element of the human condition. War was a part of the ways of society; it was considered normal in the traditions of all peoples. Every society had its warriors, and violence could be decked out in the trappings of nobility. It was violence which gave victory to a nation and crowned its leaders with glory. Violence between individuals in the form of manslaughter was part of social life. Even today

An address to the Katholikentag, Düsseldorf, 4 September 1982.

many people think of violence as a necessary part of an individual's development and of social existence.

For centuries Christianity has made the refusal of violence into a special calling; this may have been the exceptional vocation of a few but it has been fairly widespread throughout Christian peoples. It is the vocation of men and women consecrated totally to God. Just as they gave up money, so they gave up carrying swords and weapons.

They thus gave up part of their civil rights so as to be in this world the witnesses of a kingdom yet to come. It was Christianity which brought to societies based on force the notion that practical dealings between persons and countries could derive from something other than violence and war: "Blessed are the peacemakers." It was this Christian experience which enabled human beings to see that violence could become a temptation, a cause of sin springing from the human heart. This new way of looking at violence has meant that our societies have been haunted by a sort of nostalgia for a holiness which they cannot attain to; the reason is that if you want peace and if you want to give up violence you are really hankering after holiness.

The Gospel has brought into the world a longing for peace which has struck a chord in the heart of humankind, in answer to the prophecy of Isaiah who said that "they shall beat their swords into ploughshares" (Isa. 2:4). Jesus promised that he would give his peace: "peace I leave with you; my peace I give to you; not as the world gives do I give to you" (John 14:27). Since then there has been a vague hope at the heart of the masses that peace might be a possibility, that violence might be set aside. So today in our countries, and universally as the twentieth century draws to a close, a challenge is making itself felt; it is the hope for peace which seems somehow incapable of being fulfilled. Those who are cynical about the possibility of peace allege the hard facts of political reality and talk about the wisdom of the nations. And there is a greater paradox still; the desire for peace, for the giving up of violence, is being manipulated by the powers which face each other across the world so that it becomes an instrument of violence for their profit. The world cannot give peace. So how can peace be brought into the world? How can we bring forth peace? There is only one answer; we must allow ourselves to be born again in Christ and in the Holy Spirit and in mercy.

The Book of Genesis shows *division* between human beings as something universal. Does that mean that the unity of the human race is something that belongs to the distant past or to utopia? Where are we to look for equality and the respect of everyone and a communion based on justice for all? Humankind has experienced its differences as something unfortunate and yet humanity is constituted by a great variety of peoples, languages, cultures, and nations; this variety is a good thing and belongs to creation. Each individual can rejoice in the features that God gives, even though a white person's face is not the same as a black person's and even though the German language is not intelligible to French people; so also each nation should rejoice in its native identity. But in fact humanity has always experienced these as sources of division so that the identity of groups has been the cause of misunderstandings, barriers to communications, attempts to dominate, rivalries, and injustice.

If the love human beings have for self is combined with contempt for God and for others, then their special characteristics become merely the basis for their own identity instead of being also an opportunity for communion with God and with the whole of humankind. Christianity has received from Jesus the mission to make all nations into his disciples so that there will be one People of God and one Lord. This mission shows up even more starkly the divisions among human beings which spring from sin and are the cause of sin. In the heart of a divided humanity Christianity has given rise to the hope of universal peace, that hope which the Enlightenment of the eighteenth century, the *Aufklärung*, expressed as hope for a society of nations.

Now at the end of the twentieth century that hope is becoming the cause of a new temptation. The experience of the last decades has been so cruel that any thought of agreement based on justice seems illusory. Many are tempted to give up hope as if this were something that men and women can never achieve. It is in fact a great temptation to despair of the possibility of order derived from international justice when states behave like great empires and take decisions which are based on violence and greed instead of communion and justice. So one has to ask whether Christianity has been preaching something which is an illusion. Here Christianity is challenged again by something which it has itself introduced into the world, an ideal of communion and justice.

So the Christian faith has brought forth hope for humankind; at the same time Christians, and humankind as a whole, have experienced their inability to make it a reality. Today this communion in justice can appear as the dream, or the utopia, of the whole of humanity; indeed, Christian nations are not better than others in achieving the realization of that hope which they have brought forth. They are being judged by the hope which they have engendered.

If hunger, violence, and division are not the inescapable scourges of humankind, then they must issue from the heart of men and women, from their temptations and their faults. Christianity fosters the hope for sharing, peace, and unity; it also preaches that all persons are children of the same Father. Its mission is to make the one God known to all peoples. Its aim is to bring about the gathering of all in the worship of the only God, according to the message given to the prophet Isaiah. What the prophets proclaimed as belonging to the future, the Church receives as its mission for the present.

What is this hope destined to come to? Can we see any fulfillment of that promise in a world where death reigns? In Europe we had received as our inheritance that hope for the establishment of a community based on the knowledge of the one true God. But instead we experienced religious divisions, the Church separating itself from Israel, quarrels between Christians of East and West, between Catholics and Protestants. All these divisions are not the natural flowering of a variety of gifts; they brought the experience of a breakup. Faith shows us that this dramatic history is the outcome of sin and that sin is all the greater for striking at the greatest and deepest unity, the love of God. So Christianity goes on preaching unity and nourishing hope, but these refer to a communion which seems less and less accessible. If the Christian faith condemns religious hatred, does it not thereby expose humankind to the risk of despair?

If we try to avoid that risk, there is the temptation of reducing the unity promised to the children of God to some project which would be within the capacities of human nature. Or else the temptation is to dream about unity in a utopian sort of way adapted to human desires. In either case we are tempted to give up and to decide that Christian hope is illusory. We are tempted no longer to believe that Christ unites Israel and the nations into one single people. We are tempted to think that hope is deceptive just because we have not succeeded in actualizing it and because it shows up our sinfulness.

It is not hope which is deceptive because it witnesses to the fact that God is rich in mercy. Hunger, violence, division, and religious hatred are sins which issue from the human heart, and yet sharing, peace, justice, and harmony are not illusory. Even if humankind does condemn itself, God is greater than the human heart. Even if humanity is incapable of fulfilling the promises and responding to hope, God comes to meet it. It is to God that we must turn. It is to God that we must be converted.

There is however one thing that our hope is lacking. Our faith, our hope, and our charity lack the patience of history. If they had that, they would see that we reach God at the end of our pilgrimage. We lack the faith and hope in a God who is coming at the end of our own individual times and until the end of time. We fail to turn toward God as to the one whose coming and whose reign give to the time of human beings an unavoidably tenuous and precarious character. We refuse to accept that "the form of this world is passing away" (1 Cor. 7:31). We want to transfer the absolute value of God's promises to our immediate temporal achievements. So we reduce the hope that God entertains for us. While we are looking forward to short-term achievements, we allow no space for a conversion to the living and eternal God.

Our failure is that we are not feeding the world, we are not able to guarantee peace, and we are not establishing justice; nor are we bringing about unity between Christians, between all who are groping for God. We may be waiting impatiently, but our desires are selfish and are not open to the patience of God, to that charity which "bears all things and endures all things" (1 Cor. 13:7), the charity of God, our creator and redeemer.

The history of Europe in recent decades shows many traces of that distorted hope. We can see it in liberalism with its anarchy, in Nazism and its barbarity, and in communism with its imperialism. The ambition of Europe, even in its universal aims, even when they are generous aims, has distorted the hope for justice and peace and has changed them either into a utopia or into an earthly messianism. We have despaired of waiting for what is humanly impossible, but we have not had faith in what is possible to God. It is our impatience and our selfishness which are making conversion to the God of hope impossible because we want to bring sinful humanity immediately to the perfection of a justice and a peace which are outside time; this is a denial of the reality of history.

The eternal and living God accepted history when he gave to it his Son and the possibility of becoming his adopted children. So the continuous process of time has become spiritually the expression of the patience of God and the wisdom of God. It is also the time of Christ's Passion in his members and the space where the promise is being fulfilled and where salvation is being realized.

Our impatience knows nothing about the respite which God grants to human freedom so that it can come to confess its sinfulness and come to know the mercy which heals its wounds and restores hope. We have forgotten the heavenly city; how can we expect to convert our earthly cities to God? We have forgotten the eternity of the God who is love; how can we expect our history to be the bearer of his love? We do not have a future if God does not provide one for us on the last day. There can be no history without divine election and the basis of that election is the goal toward which it is tending, the *eschaton* of God. Human time therefore, the time of our freedom, our weakness, and our sinfulness, unfolds between two limits, divine election and the fulfillment of God's promises. That is why human time is also time for the mercy of God and for salvation.

Today the living and true God has come to us, his eternity fulfilling our time. The time which humanity had lost receives an opening on to the effective mercy of Christ. The times are fulfilled. God has fulfilled the promise he made to Abraham by sending his eternal Word into time. God keeps time open, and his faithfulness and the fullness of his tenderness are made manifest there. God has come to forgive. The kingdom of God has drawn near but it cannot be grasped by us; it must be established by God in the mystery of his sovereign activity which heals us and re-creates us. The kingdom of God is not something which we in our impatience can acquire and possess. Rather it is the fullness of God's patience by which he wins back his creature in love. God has come to show mercy and to welcome back the wounded freedom of humanity's children so that he can share his own life with them in his Son.

The kingdom of God is very near and the times are fulfilled. You must be converted. You must repent. Turn away from your sin. Turn to the God who forgives. That was the message of John the Baptist at the start of the Gospel; Jesus proclaims the same and the mission entrusted to the apostles by the risen Christ is the same: baptism for the forgiveness of sins. History begins to have a meaning when human persons are thus freed from sin and death, and when the love and eternity of the living God restore them to wholeness. You must be converted; turn back to God; return to the source from which comes your very existence; return to the covenant which has its roots in creation. Remember the faithfulness to which you have been called.

Conversion is the return of one who was lost and wandering in the desert; by it one returns to that original and constitutive call of God. We turn back to the living and true God when we recognize the nearness of his power and his love manifested in the Passion of his Son. So let us turn back to God as to the spring from which our existence flows. Let us go back to that point where our history begins to make sense again because it is there that we receive the mission to show forth in time the mercy of our God. Thus do the times remain opportune, a time of grace and of pardon.

Believe in the Gospel. The word *gospel* has a special meaning which is made clear by the prophet Isaiah: "How beautiful upon the mountains are the feet of him who brings good tidings, who publishes peace, who brings good tidings, who publishes salvation, who says to Sion, 'Your God reigns'" (Isa. 52:7). So the Gospel is the message about the reign of God, about his presence in the midst of his people and about his coming to those who are his own. The Gospel is the Good News that the holiness of God is granted to us in the gift of the Holy Spirit. It is by his Spirit that God makes known his kingdom, guides his people (Isa. 63:14), and makes it possible for us to be faithful to the promise. The Good News is that God gives the Holy Spirit to his servants so that they can do his will and live in the state of holiness to which he calls them. God asks for something and then he makes the fulfillment of his request possible by giving to us his own Spirit so that we are able to keep his commandments. The kingdom of God has come; believe in the Good News. The promise which God has made is yours henceforth. The fulfillment consists in the mystery of Christ and occurs when the one who has been crucified in the form of a slave gives forth the Spirit.

Believing in the Gospel does not mean accepting some blueprint which probably cannot be put into practice, nor is it dreaming about utopia. It is proclaiming that God has come to achieve in us what he himself has asked us to do. Thus in Christ our actions become a sharing in the action of God. In Christ God achieves what he says he will and he gives to us the possibility of achieving, in him and by him, what he asks for. The Good News is that in Christ humanity has allowed itself to be grasped by God, even to the depths of its freedom, since "God is at work in you both to will and to work" (Phil. 2:13). That is salvation for all the nations.

"The times are accomplished." "The kingdom of God is very near." "Be converted." "Believe in the Good News." These four sayings of Christ are really only one. They indicate that God's sovereign activity has been introduced into the world and that it is the very concrete activity of the God who works through grace. It is not for us to attempt to apply the Gospel to human situations. The whole point of the Gospel proclamation is that it is God, in Christ his anointed one, who has manifested his strength, that he acts in the depth of human freedom and that he makes it possible for us to live in the holiness of God. The Gospel witnesses to the fact that this wonder is at work through the continuing offer of salvation and the continuous granting of forgiveness. The Gospel proclaims our entry into the Resurrection of the one who was crucified; it proclaims the anticipation here and now of a universe transformed by being reconciled, a universe of which the Church is the sacrament.

The Church is the sacrament of the new world; it is the sign and witness of a universe which has been reconciled by God. The Church is made up of human beings who are hostile to each other and yet who are transferred by God into love; the Church is composed of people who are greedy for possessions and yet are brought together by God in the blessedness of the poor. Those who are in the Church are violent, yet God reconciles them in the blessedness of the peacemakers; they are unjust, yet God transforms them by his holiness; they are divided, yet God unites them in harmony. If you believe in the Gospel, then you believe in the Church; you see it as a visible manifestation of God's kingdom; you see it as a place where charity is at work and where human beings, who are by nature enemies of God and of one another, are constantly being reconciled afresh. If you believe in the Gospel, then you see the Church as the sacrament of a world renewed and the anticipation of a new humanity.

Human beings may be utterly different and opposed to one another but, when they are baptized into God's grace, they are born into the same life and they become brothers and sisters. We need that new birth, that second coming into life, in order to bring to an end the deadly quarrels between brothers and sisters. The Church is the place where those, who are still tempted by strife because of their historical condition, receive the hope of a new communion through the grace of their new birth. If you believe in the Gospel, you can see that it is in the Church that the power of the Spirit is given, the Spirit who heals and unites. If you believe in the Gospel and in the Church, then you rely on the one who calls us to reconciliation and you put your life into the hands of the one who gives himself as communion. Faith is required for all this, but faith is in fact given to us as God acting at the heart of our freedom. God's action brings forth in us the works of brothers and sisters just as it brings forth the actions of Christ. God as Father manifests his salvation because he gives to us poor sinners the capacity of accomplishing, in Christ and in his Church, those works of holiness which he creates for us.

The Church is that place of fellowship where God's power for the salvation of humankind is made manifest and reconciles. But, as history shows, the Church is made up of human beings who are greedy and violent. Christians perpetrate acts of violence and injustice. And yet all the time the Spirit is raising up men and women dedicated to justice and peace; the Spirit brings them together so that through their love of Christ they too will be able to suffer the utmost violence and thus demonstrate God's compassion. Like Father Maximilian Kolbe, they will go as far as to give up their lives for their brothers and sisters in places where sin and injustice prevail.

To the Church has been entrusted a mystery of mutual forgiveness and divine reconciliation. One has to admit that there is a spiritual dimension to what has been achieved in reconciling the bishops of Poland and of Germany, and also, I hope, the Christians of France and the Christians of Germany. When we talk about reconciliation, we are not doing so lightly, like those hypocrites who can mouth peaceful platitudes because the conflicts are over. We are deeply scarred by the wrongs that have been committed and by the sins of those who have committed them. But that sorrow, which would leave us without consolation, can come to an end if we accept the coming of a redeemer who is also a consoler. Every time we ask for forgiveness and every time we forgive and make peace, we are witnessing to a redeeming process which is being given. The one who gives it is so much greater than we are; he is our creator and our Lord and he gives us back to each other as brothers and sisters. When Christian peoples, in spite of their past history, are reconciled to one another, that is the action of God. It is an act of God which shows forth the power of that peace which has been brought by the Messiah. Thus are the people of each generation delivered from those dark powers which dwell in the secret of their heart and which they inherit from their culture.

Every act of reconciliation between Christians is an anticipation of the unity of the whole human race, the unity of the children of God. That unity remains something promised for the future, but it is also a gift by which God creates unity. God is at work, perpetually bringing together his scattered children. The unity which exists between believers in the Church is not just something which derives from a human consensus. Christian unity exists through the action of God and by his grace. It is really God who unites us when we celebrate the Eucharist. At whatever time or place we need to be reinstated into the full communion of the body of Christ, it is the action of Christ who reunites us and Christ who seizes us in his Spirit.

It is not given to humankind to achieve the unity of Christians, nor the unity of the faithful, nor the unity of the children of Adam. If you try to achieve the unity of humankind in human terms only, you are making it impossible, and that goes for Christian unity too. Unity in the deepest sense includes the hope that death will be overcome, so death and murder are major obstacles to unity. To divide human beings and to separate Christians are always an anticipation of death; it is like bringing nearer that total death which would consist in being lost forever, far away from God. It is only by God's power, which is always at work uniting in his Church both the living and the dead, that death is overcome and that the powers of hell, which are referred to in the Scriptures as Hades, are overcome.

If you are converted to the loving God, if you believe in the Gospel and do the works of God, then you are allowing God to carry out the gathering together of a divided humankind in his Church, which is both prophecy and sacrament of his kingdom. We must believe in the Church. We must work at the kingdom. We must recognize that unity of the living and the dead which God is always bringing about in Christ. The Church both proclaims and anticipates that gathering together. The gathering together of God's kingdom is stronger than death; it snatches from death and from perdition all those who are loved by God, a multitude without number of his sons and daughters.

Unity is achieved by God in his Son and by the Spirit. The Gospel shows us the cross which gathers together the four corners of the horizon. So the disciples of Christ must live out through history a unity which is centered on the Crucified One. Until the time when we can raise the triumphant song of the Apocalypse, the unity of the human race, in itself and with God, remains at the level of that hope in which we are called to believe and which nourishes our charity. At the point in the unfolding of history which is ours, that hope stretches out to infinity. The heavenly Jerusalem will only be assembled once the immense multitude of the dead and of humanity's victims has been gathered. The Jerusalem above is being constructed by the resurrection from the dead.

At present we can only hope and believe in justice and peace in unity. Christ prays that they may be realized: "may they all be one, just as, Father, you are in me and I am in you, so that they also may be in us, so that the world may believe it was you who sent me" (John 17:21). What would become of Christian faith if that prayer of Christ were ineffective? But our faith knows that the prayer of Christ is heard; Christ is always gathering us anew in the Spirit according to the will of the Father. Such a unity is grace; it is the grace of conversion. Our task today is to maintain our hope in that grace and to welcome it. It is the work of God and it is wonderful in our eyes.

The Relevance of the
Christian Message

Wouldn't you say that historically Christianity is losing ground today?

It is true that we are experiencing a very rapid evolution of social structures and of thought, which means that what was inherited from culture and tradition is being swept aside. This means that Christianity is being strongly challenged insofar as it belongs to a reality which grew up in the past, but then so are most of our social landmarks. In the present period of rapid change Christianity is losing large sections of what I would call its sociological dimensions.

In a way that is a loss because every dislocation of culture is a loss. However, one should not be too nostalgic about it because any culture which becomes static is bound to die. A living culture evolves, but evolution is risky and those cultures too are sometimes destroyed when the level of change reaches a certain threshold. It is difficult to judge one's own period. Luck comes into it. Only future generations will be able to have an objective judgment, if ever they remember what we said!

At the same time there is something positive about the situation. I have the feeling that our age is the first one since the time of ancient Rome when Christianity and its message, with all that it implies, have rung out as something new. It is as though for a thousand years Christianity has been considered as something inherited from one's ancestors. When you inherit something, it becomes part of the furniture; you don't see it anymore. Then suddenly we woke up to the fact that we were destroying an inheritance. In the early centuries Christianity challenged the different religions and cultures of Europe and of Asia; it challenged the paganism of the Mediterranean world and so its newness was obvious. Then it transformed these cultures, molded them in depth, and thereby it became identified with them. Those

An interview with Gérard Leclerc, published in *Le Quotidien*, 10–11 April 1982.

who inherited these cultures forgot that one has to *become* a Christian; they thought that Christianity was part of something one inherited.

The progress of rational thought later brought them to dissociate themselves from this inheritance, as though they were asserting their independence. Thus the progress of thought in Western Europe came partly from the fruitfulness of the biblical tradition and partly from a sort of reaction against that tradition, a claim for independence in relation to it.

Today I would say that the newness of Christianity is much clearer as it faces a new world. Rational thought is no longer a Western phenomenon; it has gained a lot by being received by all the cultures of the world and by receiving something from them. I don't think that one can say that the Japanese have become Westerners but Western scientific thought has become Japanese. So what has happened is that our mental universe has been expanded to the limits of the world. A new age has come in which we are all contemporaries, both as agents and victims. It is an age which holds out rich promise but also frightening prospects.

In this new age Christianity can at last be seen in its newness, and its freshness is evident once more. A few isolated individuals already sensed this in ages past, such as Pascal at the start of the development of modern scientific thought. The great mystics saw this too; sometimes it came to them with a terrifying rending of their inner selves; sometimes they saw it as a dazzling light to the mind as it was fascinated by the beauty of God and the harmony of the universe.

In my view this newness of Christianity is something that the new world civilization can now see. In fact there is a kind of creativity within Christianity which its traditional adherents find it difficult to come to terms with; it can be seen more clearly in new countries, new peoples, and new ways of thinking.

I believe your recent journey in Africa made a deep impression on you.

Yes, it did. Not that I think Africa is the ideal. But even in our own country the God-question is being asked again. I am not saying that the need for religion is like some vague social disease brought about by worrying times. It isn't because of increasing unemployment that attendance at mass is going to go up. The present upheaval of civilization is having the effect of an earthquake.

These earth tremors of modern culture are revealing deep layers of humanity's religious quest. Think how complacent Americans felt when the first one set foot on the moon and how self-satisfied the French were when they put up the Tour Montparnasse.[1] Compare that with what we feel today about

---

1. The Tour Montparnasse was completed in 1973 and is 656 feet high. Along with La Défense but on the Left Bank of the Seine, it is one of the few skyscrapers built in Paris. It dominates the southern skyline as seen from the center of the city. (Translator's note)

our limitations. I think that we are much more realistic today about the human condition than we were thirty or even twenty years ago. It isn't just a mood that has changed.

But if there is a kind of nihilism today, or even a devouring thirst for the sacred, that isn't necessarily going to help Christianity.

I would prefer to say that we are in a period when humankind is without bearings, especially at the level of feelings and value judgments. I am struck by how weak judgments of conscience are. Take abortion, for instance. How can you explain that public opinion swung round so completely in such a short time, according to the opinion polls anyway? How can you explain such a sudden swing in the value judgments of a whole society?

Look at the phenomenon of violence. There too one can see a complete change of public opinion. We laugh at the punk style being adopted by large sections of the population, but what we are doing is accepting violence. Do you remember how appalled people were when *Clockwork Orange* first came out? Now it's the cult of an entire generation. What I find worrying and needing an explanation is that there can be such a swing round of value judgments in our society. It could mean that the decisive questions of the difference between right and wrong had come to depend on conformity to the social milieu. Such a sociological conformity is something fragile and apt to be manipulated. As soon as conscience becomes aware that it is being reduced to social conformity, it breaks away and asserts its freedom as the ultimate principle of morality. So the modern conscience, in spite of its strength, is a conscience that does not know the difference between right and wrong any longer.

So what you are saying about our civilization is really the same as Solzhenitsyn.

It is the basic question. Humankind is lost if it does not know the difference between right and wrong. The power of the Christian message, the impact of someone like Pope John Paul, for instance, as far as nonbelievers are concerned stems from the fact that they spell out humanity's condition by indicating what is good for it and what is evil for it. To be able to do this, it is not sufficient to recite by heart a catechism of simple answers. When Christians utter their message, they know that they must prepare for conflict. That conflict basically is the power of God at work in setting humankind free.

If modern man and woman were to be given a clear view of their own dignity, they would be in the process of becoming free. But anyone who speaks that sort of language is opening up himself or herself to the cross because these truths are hard to bear. However, such a price must be paid if humankind is to be set free and saved.

If we are looking for a pseudoscientific justification for a person's basic rights, we will soon fall into grave error, whether that justification is decked out with the trappings of the social sciences, biology, physics, or productivity. Our age, precisely because it is so powerful, must discover the signposts which will show it the way. That is why I think that Christianity is so up-to-date, not because it will ever become fashionable, but because it brings the truth with all its demands.

What If the Church Were Ahead in Matters of Morals?

The future of Christianity is not being decided in our Western countries only. Look at the upsurge of life in Asia, Africa, South America, and even in the United States. When I meet French missionaries, both priests and lay people, from these countries, they often say to me when they come back to France: "Things are just dead round here!"

Isn't that rather a bleak outlook for the West?

I am certainly not the first to say that there is a long drawn-out spiritual crisis in Western Europe and especially in France. Since the nineteenth century, many people have been saying that, from Rimbaud to Léon Bloy. That's what the generation of May 1968 was saying in its own way. However, we are now living through a time which is less sure of itself than the fifties and sixties. At least today fundamental questions are coming up again. It seems to me that we are moving into a period that is more open and where ready-made views of Christianity have less hold on people's minds. People don't hold an archbishop in awe, any more than they do a member of the French Academy. But they are asking questions about the meaning of their life and they are saying to Christians: "speak up if you have something to say." That's new.

But what isn't very new, however, is the kind of answer that the highest authorities in the Church are giving on questions of day-to-day morality, such as sexuality!

The prevailing climate we live in is very uncertain. If we Christians were saying that "on these questions we should follow the prevailing climate and the current views," we would probably commit the same mistakes as those who are trying to solve immigration problems with bulldozers.

Interview with Gérard Dupuy and Luc Rosenzweig, published in *Libération,* 27 September 1983.

16

So we must distinguish three things: first, the mores of a society, what most people consider right at a given time and place; second, current legislation on moral matters; third, the moral judgment of an enlightened conscience on what is true and good.

There has always been a gap between these three aspects. Take, for instance, the history of sexual mores in Europe. For centuries concubinage was prevalent, though it was never legal. During the nineteenth century, and even later, it was normal in France for young men from the middle class to have a mistress before marriage. So one must not be naive and think that the gap between mores, the law, and moral judgment has never occurred before our time. . . .

Let us come back to the present. I am certain that the Catholic Church, with its hard line on sexuality, is uttering a warning cry to the whole of society on the way sex and the body are being used. What has happened currently is that sexuality has been assimilated to any other consumer goods. Why? Because sexuality is reduced to sexual desire and desire is treated as a source of profit. It must be aroused so that there can be a sale. Gradually, as the erotic sector of the market grows, whole areas of public morality are being eroded.

What the Catholic Church is doing is reminding people that this whole area, which our culture is trying to remove from the moral sphere, is subject to the requirements of morality. In consequence, the Church appears to be isolated and to be swimming against the tide. Naturally such a stance requires a lot of courage. But what the Church is doing is forcing people to think more deeply about the following questions: What is the nature of the human body? What is the reason for its dignity in sexual relations and more generally in social life? What is the nature of the relation between men and women? What part does enjoyment play in free choice? All these questions raise major issues about the way the whole of society works. So the Church is forcing society to look at these vital issues. . . .

But isn't it true that the Church's condemnation of certain practices, like homosexuality for instance, can be very hurtful for the people concerned?

You are raising a very important question which does not concern only homosexuality but the whole area of ethics. In morality, if you have a general and objective judgment about what is right, that is not the same thing as judging an individual case. If you say something general about homosexuality, that is not the same thing as condemning a homosexual. What you are saying in a general and objective statement on sexual morality is concerned wtih the aims of creation. Take another example: you would not say that a condemnation of theft and murder automatically entailed the execution of the thief and the murderer. The Church can blame a certain type of activity without outlawing human beings. It is one thing to be tolerant of deviation to the point of permissiveness; it is another thing to respect every human being, whoever he or she may be. Anyway, even if society condemns someone as a deviant, the Church does not consider any individual as deviant or marginal forever, because the Church believes in the possibility of salvation for everyone.

However, the changing of legislation in relation to deviant sexual behavior is a matter which carries with it a serious responsibility. If deviant behavior comes to be considered as normal just because the law was ill adapted to cope with it, what happens is that the lawgiver no longer helps individuals to fulfill their responsibility; on the contrary, their capacity for moral resistance is weakened and, in the end, their freedom is weakened. Really, where sexual morality is concerned, I would be inclined to adopt a point of view inherited from the past, because what it does basically is remind us of a fundamental requirement of moral behavior, which is that a general norm eventually frees even those subject to particular failings.

I think that there is a similarity here with the position taken up by the Church on problems of labor. In his encyclical letter *Laborem Exercens* the pope said that we must put human beings back at the center of the economic system; many people are returning to that point of view. On the question of sexuality and attitudes to the body, society is today more or less where it was a hundred years ago in social matters. In the nineteenth century capitalism was rampant and factories were exploiting child labor. In the twentieth century it is being exploited for sexual ends. There has been a kind of erotic explosion which justifies that sort of behavior and it comes from the application of modern science to sexuality. This produces excesses in sexual matters which are rather like the excesses produced at the beginning of the industrial revolution. So it seems as though the Church, in its attitude to the human body, is not lagging behind but is well ahead.

Humankind without a Goal: Our Contemporary Paradox

Many political and economic problems are basically cultural problems. Such is the case with the problems which are the subject of political debate in France: our educational system, the birthrate, human control over life and death, the question of world hunger and the standard of living, peace and peace protests, solidarity and work sharing. All these acute problems stem from our cultural situation because we do not control the forces at work in it, nor can we analyze them adequately, nor can we tell in advance what technological approaches are going to be required. By culture I do not mean only or even primarily what is produced by cultural activity; I mean by it something which lies behind cultural activity. I mean the way in which humankind can fashion the world it lives in and the way in which it can contribute to the creation of humanity.

Anyone who analyzes the situation must come to the conclusion that we are at the end of an epoch. The time from the beginning of the nineteenth century to now I consider to have been one period because it was then that humanity undertook something phenomenal; it undertook to define its own goals and to give itself the means of reaching them. This undertaking was based on the independence of human development and on the unfettered use of reason which was responsible to itself alone; but it implied more. It implied the conquest of the material world and also the conquest of its spiritual dimension and, even more than that, the conquest of humankind itself. Humankind became its own goal and also the means for that attainment. One should not reduce this undertaking to those things which were either the means it used or the consequences it produced; such were the new techniques made possible by technology, the enormous production of natural wealth, the control of natural environment, the insane stockpiling of arma-

An article published in *Études*, October 1983.

ments, and so on. All these are but the manifestation of the unlimited ambition of modernity to create its own goals—freedom, prosperity, power, independence. Such goals have become so evidently desirable that the West has been able to export them irresistibly to the rest of the world. We have imposed them by a sort of colonialism which is essentially cultural and which was perhaps in that sense inevitable.

What Is at Stake in Today's Culture?

Something extraordinary is now taking place and disturbing humankind more and more. The goals which humankind had set itself are becoming a problem for it. I must make myself clear on this. It is not because humankind did not have the knowledge or the power to attain these goals, which it had set as norms for its own activity, that they have become a problem; on the contrary, it has to a large extent reached these goals. The problem is that they can now be seen to be insufficient and perverse, if not actually contradictory. We can see now that the goals which humankind has reached are incapable of ensuring its humanity. The very ends which used to appear the highest and most desirable have become either suspect or not worth having. I am reminded of Nietzsche's poem *Thus Spake Zarathustra* where he speaks of the "one thousand and one goals" which humankind comes across, which it creates and discards. Each of them is produced by the "will to power." They reflect it and are its symptoms. But none of them is able to transcend the will to power; they cannot give it a foundation nor free it from itself. We used to think that the ends we had established could really prove sufficient, that these goals which had been produced by us could really guide us in return. Now we are finding out that, precisely because they come from us in the first place, they cannot guide us to our deeper selves, that is, beyond ourselves. Pascal had said it already: "man goes infinitely beyond man."

That is the whole issue which has to be faced in today's culture. What is it in humankind that goes infinitely beyond itself? As long as it is able to define its own goals, humankind is maintaining that it is equal to itself, and so is displaying a fundamental tautology. I would like to suggest that one finds everywhere in today's culture this model of tautology: the human *ego* equals nothing but itself. Thus formal logic today seeks statements that have no real content; it recognizes as unconditionally true only purely tautological statements. Social and economic studies are at a premium and they seek states of measurable equilibrium. In psychology therapeutic methods try to achieve psychic harmony, that is, consciousness as equal to itself (Maurice Clavel used to be devastatingly sarcastic about such equilibrium).[1] Military strat-

1. Maurice Clavel (1920–79) was a French philosopher and journalist who criticized both the Marxist left and the conservatives in the name of the Christian faith. (Translator's note)

egies aim at an equilibrium of terror and this is a false imitation of the gift of universal peace. In history one finds the myth of a classless society or the idea that we can reach the frontier of a process of eternal return; it is a sort of entropy of history. I could multiply such examples which illustrate humankind's ambition to return to itself. I use the word *return* in its several meanings: it is a return to human origins; humankind belongs to itself as its inheritance; it corresponds to its idea of itself without any other dimension.

It is always being said that our civilization is based on mathematical knowledge and that is perfectly true. But one should accept the consequences of this. Mathematics is abstract; it only claims to explore the complex structures of those similarities which the human mind can master. One could say that it is a sophisticated analysis of tautology. It is completely outside the scope of mathematics to identify ends and to reach conclusions which transcend the data at the start of a process. Nowadays we are beginning to discover that tautology is not always possible; the learning model which is based on absolute equations is being disturbed more and more by the complexity of whatever reality it is considering. The difficulties experienced by economics and the social sciences in setting themselves up as true science make that evident. It is not always a good thing to be equated with science because the equation of identity does not, by definition, make it possible to discover a goal but only to reiterate the initial data. And yet the narcissistic tendencies of modern human beings are becoming impossible and unbearable at the same time. They have often been a temptation for humankind in the past, as shown by the words of James in his epistle: "if anyone is a hearer of the word and not a doer, he is like a man who observes his natural face in a mirror; for he observes himself and goes away and at once forgets what he was like. But he who looks into the perfect law, the law of liberty, and perseveres, being no hearer that forgets but a doer that acts, he shall be blessed in his doing" (James 1:23–25).

Transcendent Ends

If there is a crisis concerning the purpose of human actions and if that crisis comes because humankind is trying to fix its own goals by itself and for itself, then the solution is to discover, if we can, aims which transcend humankind. Transcendence is thus a necessity. We cannot consider aims which we have set ourselves as being an authentic goal. An absolute finality which is properly unconditional must both transcend us and precede us. What we must do is something quite different and quite difficult; we must accept as given a goal to our actions which we do not ourselves create. We must accept that humanity has a meaning and perspectives which we do not control and which cannot be discovered by humanism (I would prefer to call it our modern *anti*-humanism). If we are prepared to do that, then we can rediscover the question: "What does it mean to be human?" Here we sense that too rapid an answer will not do. It would be like trying to fill the gap which is opening by some ready-made answer. Such a question needs to be contemplated in silence so that it can be asked correctly and can mature. If that happens, we can begin to sense that the difficulty we have in answering gives us a clue as to what is at stake. If humankind cannot give an adequate definition of itself, this could indicate that, like God, it does not have a definition. The fact that humankind and God cannot be defined points to a likeness between them. I am thinking of what Gregory of Nyssa said: the human being is created in the image and likeness of the unknowable God; therefore humankind is unknowable because of its unrevealed finality. So perhaps we have here the great cultural breakthrough of the last few years. Modern human beings are coming to realize that their humanity transcends whatever understanding they may have of it; and they are coming to see that the end to which humankind is tending cannot be produced by itself, any more than it could create itself at the beginning.

It would be possible to confirm the foregoing analysis by adverting to the numerous crises occurring before our very eyes—all connected with matters of finality. Each time we can see the end, to which a whole series of human actions is tending, eluding humanity's grasp at the very moment when it seems at the point of being reached. Thus the development of technology by its very success produces such a concentration and specialization of labor that it causes underdevelopment and famine for a growing number of human beings. Medicine and the human sciences try sincerely and explicitly to promote health and life, but they are now capable of manipulating human beings to such an extent that decisions are made administratively about life and death or about development which effectively reduce human beings to the level of livestock. The demand for freedom is in itself something fundamentally good, but it produces all sorts of slavery for humankind if it yields to various irrational forms of deviation and anarchy. I could give any number of examples, but I will restrict myself to the one that is most significant, the crisis of our educational system. I do not mean by this tensions between the generations or reforming our schools; I mean the real crisis of which these are the clear symptoms. What is happening is that young people in most Western countries and in the Soviet bloc are refusing to accept the aims and values of the society they live in. Such a refusal of tradition indicates that these societies will not be able to survive; the basic requirement of social living, which is the process by which younger generations take up ancient challenges, is being met with increasing difficulty. This is a crisis which concerns the goals which humankind has set for itself. But young people are refusing them because these goals imply a self-regarding narcissism which is a form of suicide. So what the younger generation is doing is witnessing, often without knowing it clearly, to the need for a goal which is transcendent. The ideology of progress is not working anymore. History is rising up in rebellion against history if it is to be merely something humanly manufactured.

We should try to understand the significance of contemporary culture, for what it indicates is both a strange paradox and a premonition of death. Our century is discovering with horror that liberation, even when it is completely justified, can take place at the cost of dreadful injustice in the political, economic, biological, and moral spheres. There has never been a greater increase of servitude, even among the citizens of free countries and in the name of freedom itself. Our culture, as it evolves, is forcing us into a paradoxical situation. If moral freedom claims to operate according to its own rules alone, according to the dictates of autonomous reason, then it is condemning itself to ruin; we can see this happening time and time again and in all sorts of ways. If we want to rediscover the true inner laws of morality, we must go through a stage where morality submits to something other than itself; that does not mean the enslavement of moral judgment. It means that it humbly accepts the demands of our interior life and that it respects others as fellow human beings. We are beginning to take this in because so many great men and women have repeatedly witnessed to it; some have been dissidents like Solzhenitsyn and Zinoviev[2]; some are philosophers like Emmanuel Lévinas[3]; others have done great things in the field of charity and welfare like Mother Teresa, and so many others whose work remains hidden. This submission of the moral judgment is in fact an opening of oneself to the Wholly Other who transcends us and goes before us. This is the condition of our freedom since we can apply to freedom the words which Christ spoke of life itself: "whoever would save his life will lose it; and whoever loses his life for my sake and the gospel's will save it" (Mark 8:35).

The Cultural Task of Christians

Today it is the Church, as bearer of the words of Christ, which proclaims in our present crisis the reality of our humanity. It is faith which maintains Christians in love and enables them to witness to the truth in the midst of a human race which is in a state of uncertainty about its identity and about its goals. By that faith, which God's universal grace produces at the heart of our freedom, some human beings accept to lose their lives for the love of God and for the love of humanity's transcendent value. These are two aspects of the love which is poured out in our hearts. The Church speaks up for the love of love. It is faith which gives it the freedom to listen to God and to serve

2. Alexander Zinoviev (b. 1920) is a Russian philosopher of logic and the role of language in contemporary culture. After the publication in 1976 of *Les hauteurs béantes,* he was forced to leave the Soviet Union and now teaches in Munich. (Alexander Zinoviev should not be confused with Zinoviev, one of the first bolsheviks and a victim of Stalin's purge in 1934.) (Translator's note)

3. Emmanuel Lévinas (b. 1905 in Lithuania) is a French Jewish philosopher who popularized the thought of Husserl and Heidegger in France. (Translator's note)

humanity's transcendent goal. It has to do this in the midst of societies, pressure groups, and political or military powers which cannot escape from the iron necessity of trying to ensure their own survival by purely inward-looking achievements. Christians on the other hand do not stand to lose money or power or positions of influence, nor cultural mastery, the reason being that they can exercise freedom in relation to ends which are considered as absolutes by those whose endeavors are limited to this world. It is the witness of Christians, a witness until death if needs be, which gives experimental evidence that there is another goal which makes human fulfillment possible. This witness rescues us from a suicidal imprisonment within our own limits. The freedom which Christians receive from God gives them a decisive role in the struggle which is being waged for humanity. It appears to be a desperate struggle to anyone observing the crisis of contemporary culture. But to the disciple that struggle is full of a hope which cannot be quenched because the disciple who has followed in the footsteps of the Son of Man has received a revelation of what the human condition really is.

The role which Christians have in today's culture is to be the witness of the transcendent goal of humankind. In Christ, God proposed to us a pattern whereby we can discover ourselves. It is the image and likeness not of what we could imagine as the greatest but of God himself. It is the mystery of paternity and filiation in love. During the nineteenth century Christianity was in the dock while a case was being brought against it in the name of humankind; it was a long and hard trial. But now the roles are different; it is Christianity which is pleading, silently and insistently, on behalf of humankind and against a false autonomy which would reduce us to being only such as we can imagine. It is Christianity which has become humankind's advocate, since it has often been stripped of its humanity by the very ones who should have bestowed it. Christianity does not press the indictment; all it does is display the face of Christ, a man accused and put to death, as that of true humanity. This truth about humankind was promised to it when it was created and when it was called to divine adoption. Adam, who stands for humankind as such, did not recognize the promises which God, in renewing the covenant with him, repeatedly offered. Adam did not recognize the divine promises and, having thus lost his true humanity, can only recover it in the Second Adam. It is in Christ that humanity discovers itself both as reconciled and as restored to its original condition. For, when they tortured Christ, men did not succeed in degrading him as men and women succeed in degrading themselves every day. Humanity appears disfigured on the face of the God-Man who has been blasphemed, but it is still an authentic humanity, so that Christ bears on his sacred countenance the reflection of the light which shone on humankind in its original state as well as the restoration of our disfigured features and the grace of our achievements. Christ is open to the love of God and open to the whole of humankind by that love; he is thus able to carry our humanity through the gates of death to our last destiny. In the words of Pilate, spoken more truly than he realized (John 19:6), *Ecce homo:* Behold *the* Human Being. Behold *Humankind.* Today Christ is the truth of humanity.

Gospel and Inculturation

The foregoing analysis has its implication for mission. If the Church of Christ is speaking on behalf of humankind in defense of its true humanity, then the relation between the Church and cultural life cannot be one of opposition, nor on the other hand can the Church connive in all the aspects of a culture. The relation of the Church to different cultures, insofar as they are the historical realizations of our fundamental calling, is different; it could be described as assimilation and fertilization. Does this mean that the Church becomes too closely linked to the different cultures? Isn't this a problem for the universality of the Church? Does inculturation not contradict all claims to universality?

If one sees a conflict between the universality of the Gospel and inculturation, it could be because one has in mind a particular pattern: one supposes that Christianity, having originated in one culture, the Semitic culture, is ceaselessly faced with other cultures (hellenistic, Latin, "barbarian") in which it must ever be implanted if it is not to disappear. Such a view reduces Christianity to being a protean entity, with only a minimal and almost indefinable element of continuity, which is constantly being assimilated and compromised by a succession of different cultures without which it would rapidly become obsolete. It is a matter of adapting or perishing. According to such a point of view, the basic reality underlying both culture and Christianity would be the society which produces cultural objects, exchanges them, and consumes them. But in fact the basic reality consists of human beings, not so much as those who produce culture and benefit from it, but as those who are revealed to the believer by God as the purpose for which culture exists. By means of the Church, Christ himself intervenes in human history. Christ in his concrete and historical identity is able to be universal and to exist "for all nations." It is the existence of the Holy Spirit which throws light on this apparent contradiction, since it is the Holy Spirit who opens to Christ human hearts and our desires in all their diversity; it is the Spirit who calls forth the faith throughout all the different cultures. Within the universal Church, the Spirit of Christ also makes particular churches develop as real expressions of the sonship of the one Father. What is more, this assimilation and fertilization of humanity by the Gospel is a cultural phenomenon. Cultures are not seen by faith as something ready-made, distant and foreign to the Church; we see them rather as produced by the fatherly foresight of God. So the proclamation of the Gospel is seen to have been anticipated providentially by something present in those cultures; when they are converted to God, then they are delivered from their servitude and their resources are enriched. That is how new cultures are born; they are brought into the world by the universal Church and they become the source of the life and character of the local churches.

I do not want to play down the crises which have occurred in history. Christians are human beings with all the limitations and the selfishness of the cultures to which they belonged. Too often they have abandoned the universal implications of their faith and have given undue importance to their own way of thinking and living. But all this hostility between nations and the limitations of particular cultures must not be allowed to mask catholicity, that is, the openness which is essential to the Gospel. The Gospel of God cannot of its very nature deny the cultures of humankind since it elevates, even to the point of resurrection, human beings who are trying through culture to accede to a better humanity.

The problem of inculturation does not lie therefore in the careful measuring out of the elements from different cultures which can be combined while respecting the Gospel and human beings. Our task as Christians is to work at such a deep evangelization under God that the phenomenon of culture is fully accepted; once that happens the men and women of various cultures will have the energy and the joy they need to overcome the failures and the shortcomings of that culture. It is not just that the faith has to give up old ways which have become obsolete so as to adapt to new languages and new cultures; but the Christian is invited by his or her faith to discern that something ever new is happening within the languages and cultures of humanity. This "happening" is the coming of the Spirit of the Messiah which has been promised to humankind so that in God it can fulfill its humanity. The Spirit who hovered over the waters at the beginning of creation now joins forces with humankind as it strives to dominate and to improve nature, as well as its own humanity. It is the Holy Spirit who helps men and women in their searching, who lifts them up after their failures, who watches over their rituals and gives power to their utterances, who fulfills them according to their hopes so that they can celebrate God's grace within the Church. There are many different manifestations of all this, just as the social and historical conditions of human existence differ; but they all converge by means of the faith on the one who calls human beings into communion. The universal catholicity of the Church always remains a possibility. In fact it becomes a reality as the result of the effective operation of the Spirit of Christ who causes the praise of the one and only Father to go up from all the ends of the earth and in all the languages of humankind. So the inculturation of the Gospel does not take place through the opposition of the faith of the Church on one side and various human cultures on the other. What occurs is the fulfillment in the faith of the promises made to humankind at the time of its creation. In the midst of their work for culture, certain men and women hear the call which fulfills them by opening them to the Christ-event and to Christ's Church. This new communion effects in them, and for their brothers and sisters, a renewal of humanity and hence a renewal of culture. This is a costly process, but that is what the Gospel and the human condition are worth; if it takes place, then the result is the inculturation of the faith and the renewal of communion among men and women. The inculturation of the Gospel produced by the Holy Spirit is like a eucharistic sacrifice and a transubstantiation.

Christ is the redeemer of humankind. In their witness to Christ, the Spirit and the Church are saying something about being human. In attesting to the reality of the salvation wrought by God, the Church shows forth to us that hope does not deceive. God is faithful; it is he who gives to us the possibility of being able to have hope in his own humanity.

God Loves Humankind

The pastors of Christ's Church exercise in his name a ministry to their brothers and sisters. That is a witness to the one who saves us and who gives to us the capacity of building our own humanity. The one who preaches the Gospel also indicates to the sons and daughters of God the ways in which they can be fulfilled as children of Adam. Those ways are means to liberty and culture. The one who gives to us for our salvation the Body and Blood of Christ in communion bestows on us the gift of unity. This helps us to work for the unity of the whole human race, a unity which is always being threatened, just as it never ceases to be an object of hope. Such is the task of the Church of God today, as it was in the past and will be in the future, in the realm of civilization and culture.

The task of a bishop is not primarily cultural; it comes to him from on high. But as pastor he would not be a witness to the mercy of God and to God's love for humankind if he did not share fully in the effort of humankind to promote and enrich its condition.

The World's Problems Are
Spiritual Problems

Y̶ou spoke of nihilism. . . .
      Yes. I see it as being the result of our helplessness when faced with the tragedy of our times: the excessive stockpiling of means of destruction, apparently unavoidable natural phenomena, such as the drought in Africa. We are told how many million people are going to die; experts say, "We don't believe in relief anymore; we can't do anything. The means aren't there. There's no political will, only corruption."

I say: no, one cannot accept such a thing. Accepting defeat is not a technical decision; it is a moral decision. The overriding moral duty is to save men, women, and children who are going to die.

There's a similar question. You are saying that all this could swing over into nihilism. But nihilism could thrive on the idea that this world is completely and utterly bad from two points of view: bad because of its totalitarian tendencies or bad because of its liberal tendencies. Now this latter reason for condemnation seems to be dominant in the Church today. Is it?

Well, you are referring to a strategic situation where some countries do not have civil liberties and where some countries do. I don't think you can equate them. You cannot equate a fixed and unchanging society based on a totalitarian ideology with societies where free interaction and internal opposition are still possible. But of course this does not mean that one sort of society commits all the faults and that the other sort is blameless.

In the present situation with its temptation to despair, what do you think the Church can do? Has she grown weary through centuries of struggle?

An interview with Olivier Chevrillon, Jacques Duquesne, and Georges Suffert, published in *Le Point,* 23 April 1984.

That's more or less the question that Stalin asked: "How many divisions has the pope?" Forgive the comparison. Let's have a look at what is going on. In a way the Church cuts across most of the conflicts in today's world. I mean by that, it can look as if it belonged to several camps, and even as if it played a double game. I can give you a personal example which goes back to the Algerian War. I was a student chaplain at the time and we had organized a mass at the Cathedral of Notre-Dame de Paris to pray for peace. I said to the students: "Our Christian faith cannot remain an empty phrase when there's a conflict going on which is tearing French people apart. I want you to make an act of faith and to believe that it is possible for enemies to pray together, not by declaring a truce, not by ignoring the problems, but because the faith creates between us a common language." There were students from both sides; I remember seeing two of them in my study, one after the other. One was on the side of French Algeria; the other supported Algerian independence. Those two lads of twenty broke down and wept because they thought their pals were going to see them as traitors, willing to treat with the enemy. But they both agreed to come to the mass. Then I tried to find adult politicians who would agree to come and pray publicly. I only managed to get three, Bidault, Michelet, and Mauriac. I shan't tell you the names of the ones who refused. But what I am saying in giving you that example is that we Christians have a freedom of language and a possibility of communication which cut across the present lineup of problems.

I can give you another example which may appear rather insignificant in relation to the problems of the world. Recently I was at the Synod of Bishops in Rome and we broke up into language groups. In the French-speaking language group the majority of bishops were African and, of the ten bishops from Africa, only two were whites. Similarly, the pope has just appointed a black cardinal to be in charge of the nomination of bishops for the whole world. So you can see in the actual workings of the Catholic Church an equality emerging which cuts across the enormous economic differences of the various parts of the world, and the apparent cultural differences too. So we are anticipating an equality which is not yet established where political societies are concerned. For fifty years the popes have been recommending something which seems like a utopia to many people and which is hardly operative at the practical level. De Gaulle used to refer to it as the "whatsit"; it is the idea of an international order which substitutes law for power as the basis for relations between states. It could be a utopia, but it could also be a reasonable anticipation of the future based on an act of faith; this is how things *could* be. What faith is saying is that rights should regulate relations between people, that rights are founded on morality, and that morality recognizes the equal dignity of all persons. Even if facts never correspond completely to rights, that does not mean that rights do not exist nor that they have no power to compel.

There's something that strikes me since we started talking. You are saying that the problems facing society are symbolic ones and that therefore they are religious ones, but you seem to equate religious and Christian. What about the other symbolic systems?

Wait a minute! Jewish and Christian symbolism are found at the heart of religious symbolism. That is a fundamental historical reality. Other symbolic systems make their contribution, but I maintain that the fundamental problems of modern society are problems of which Christianity reveals the meaning.

World civilization has been shaped by instruments of thought and by concepts which derive directly from the Jewish and Christian tradition. If you don't accept that hypothesis, there's only one other explanation, which Chamberlain puts forward in *The Foundations of the Nineteenth Century,* and that is the superiority of the white race. Why is that? Because the world is run today by modern technology, which is the same the world over, regardless of local cultures. This universality of science stems directly from a certain relation of man to creation. Now this universal instrument comes from that part of humanity which has been enriched by revelation; I don't think that's a coincidence. Take another example: Europeans discovered the rest of the world and not the other way around. So, in other words, the idea that the whole of our planet had to be inventoried is greater than the myth of a primordial man.

The Judeo-Christian tradition carries with it the hope and the ultimate vision that the human race has in fact one single fundamental origin, even though it is so divided and so diverse. The idea of universal law does not come from the Greeks; in fact it goes against the constants of ancient laws. The only thing that justifies it is the creation of all persons in the likeness of God.

Without wanting to labor the point, I repeat that all the world's problems are basically spiritual problems and that they stem from the temptations of Christianity. From this comes the inevitable conclusion that if the world's problems are spiritual problems, then there are Christian answers to the world crisis. I do not derive a sort of spiritual imperialism from this but I point to the evidence for a paradox: the main problems which constitute our world crisis (starvation, underdevelopment, wars, etc.) are capable of a technical solution. We could, *if we really wanted,* feed the whole of humanity, develop all the Third World countries, and stop the arms race. But in fact, if we do not have the technical means for this at hand, it is because we do not really want these ultimately desirable objectives. So what is making them impossible to reach now is something in our own hearts and wills. So either the real answers to the crisis are spiritual ones or there are no answers. The future of the society of the human race thus depends ultimately on love.

What you are saying is exactly the sort of thing that inspired those who formulated the social doctrine of the Church in the nineteenth century.

Exactly, but the social doctrine of the Church has not expired. It was formulated in the cultural and social conditions of the nineteenth century and so naturally it has to be restated in terms adapted to the end of the twentieth century. But that is exactly what is being done. The task of Christians is not to solve problems in the place of other people. It would be absurd to substitute Christianity for reason as a means of solving scientific, social, economic, or political problems. But to a certain extent these problems are not just due to technical shortcomings; they have at their heart a spiritual blockage and, to that extent, the holiness or lack of it of those involved, Christians and non-Christians, will make a big difference to the future of the human race.

So to summarize what you are saying: we are living in a world where more and more people are saying that there is no solution. Christians are those who come along and say "I have the solution."

No, they don't say "I have the solution." But they say "There is a solution." Can I refer you to the speech of the pope to the young people of Czechoslovakia: "It is wrong to think that there are any situations without any way out; it is wrong to say that humankind can be without a way out." Of course it can happen that the way out goes by a route where there is no immediate solution from the human point of view. But that is when a strong faith places its hope in God rather than ourselves; it maintains hope in the reality of life even when we are going through the ordeal of death; it affirms the existence of liberty even when we are subjected to the ordeal of prison. If we manage to hold fast and to remain faithful to God in the hope that there will be a way out, even when we have before us the evidence that there is no way out, then the door of our prison is already ajar.

Take the example of Poland. Youth over there has no civil liberties. The Church says to them: "Do not rise in a bloody revolution; you will only get yourselves killed for nothing. But you must not resign yourselves to your fate either. You must continue to believe in what you should believe in, freedom, your own dignity, respect for all people. So, although you are in a situation with no way out, keep alive the hope that there is an open door. Not only will it open one day, but it is opened here and now by your act of faith." That's the nature of the challenge. If Christians in Poland give way to weariness, if they accept as the only two alternatives that "either I do what everyone else is doing or else I emigrate," then there will be no way out. They will be swept aside and wiped off the world map, at least for this generation. But if they hold fast, then they have already won.

So, if all those apparently insoluble problems of the world are actually spiritual problems, then our responsibility is to dare.

In the last resort the best guarantee of our freedom and of our dignity is the desire for holiness. I would not claim that Christians or church people are always the bravest when facing events, but what I do believe is that there will always be some such people and that Christians will be among their number.

Christianity and Human Rights

Your Excellency, Archbishop Hickey, Father Byron, Reverend Fathers, Brothers and Sisters, Ladies and Gentlemen:

Allow me to tackle the question of human rights from a nontheoretical but concrete and empirical point of view.

I do not mean that the theoretical debate is uninteresting. However, we all see that there always remains a gap between theoretical conclusions and the facts that everyone experiences. This leads to a sort of skepticism and misgivings toward rationality which, I think, is most dangerous. This gap seems to have been widening in modern history. Practically all nations in the world claim to stand for human rights. But such noble principles are used to justify the most revolting abuses. The notion of human rights belongs to the universal consciousness. In the fields of social and political relationships, it is spontaneously considered as the root of the dignity of every human being; it is seen as characteristic of all human creatures. And yet all the powers in this world fight each other in the name of these very same rights, claiming that they are defending and promoting them. The sad result is that people are confused and wonder whether it is at all possible to assert anything valid and fruitful about these fundamental rights. The temptation is then to say that what is supposed to be the foundation of modern civilization (and especially that of the West), in other words, the defense of human rights, is nothing but a lie, inasmuch as it becomes an excuse for other pursuits which are certainly less respectable.

Such is the suspicion which weighs upon our Western civilization and upsets its political rationality: our most noble principles seem to be mere tools in merciless economic wars; they become weapons for what is called

An address given at The Catholic University of America, Monday, 28 April 1986, translated by Jean Duchesne.

class struggle. In our times, these misgivings on the universality of reason have engineered one of the most serious crises of political thought; they gave birth to totalitarian, revolutionary theories which claim to defend the authentic rights of the oppressed, against all kinds of alienation.

I insist that this is a lethal crisis, because it affects not only the West but also the whole world. The stage for this tragedy is not confined merely to Europe in the twentieth century, because the ideological conflict now draws lines across all continents. And it is not only the West against the East, nor even (perhaps) the North against the South. No: it's worse. The suspicion now undermines any civilized consciousness. The question is: Can anything trustworthy and decisive be said about humankind? Is there a rationality which might give way to universal ethical principles? In which field of human knowledge is such a rationality to be found?

To us, Europeans, and consequently also to you, Americans, the question was asked most brutally during the last world war. Let me take no more than two significant examples.

The first is medical experiments in Nazi concentration camps. I need not and I do not wish to recall sickening details. I shall make but one point: at Nuremberg, when these doctors were tried, the most amazing discovery was that they were not all sadists and madmen. But many of them were standard university professors, scientists, and researchers, following the usual norms and rules of scientific ethics and rationality, trying to solve problems which today remain unsolved and which the scientific community keeps on coping with according to the same theoretical or epistemological principles. The Nazi doctors obviously went too far and forgot other moral principles. But the point is that, at Nuremberg, their guilt or innocence was determined on the basis of the consequences of what they had done, because of the revulsion their work produced. But the underlying principles which made such horrors possible were not even examined.

What remains after the Nuremberg trials is that we do not know for sure what human beings can and cannot do with their bodies, what bodily integrity and individual identity actually mean. Even if it can be positively defined, even if there are constitutionally binding decisions (like the ones of the United States Supreme Court or those in other democracies), yet there seems to be no absolute rule that binds the conscience of all human beings. No court sentence can instantaneously make good what is felt to be bad, or bad what is thought to be good. The question remains unanswered: How to found human rights rationally?

May I be so bold as to remind you that this was precisely the ambition of your founding fathers? Yours, and also ours, the founders of modern civilization. Our common hope, the faith of all civilized nations has been and remains that reason can provide firm ground to establish what it means to be human and what the fundamental civil and human rights are. This assumption has allowed us to live and our fathers have died for it. But is it really clear to us?

The other example I want to mention is still a painful recollection for Europeans. And I know it is no less agonizing here in America. I mean the strange balance and alliance of forces which allowed the Nazi tyranny to be overcome. For us Europeans, suffering under Hitler's occupation, the Allied forces were the defenders of liberty. And especially the Americans were our liberators. As soon as we learned that the United States was waging war, we knew for sure that victory was certain and we also felt that this would be the triumph of justice and freedom. America at war meant that moral concerns were once again part of a struggle which so far had seemed meaningless. We knew at once that all this meant that "might is not right." It was like a compensation and forgiveness for the political sin of the weakness of European democracies, which let Poland be torn to pieces, allowed Czechoslovakia to disappear, tolerated the *Anschluss* of Austria, and suffered the shame of Munich before the puzzled eyes of the world's conscience.

I am not speaking as a historian or as a politician, but as a witness of all these events. I then was a teenager and fully aware of all that was at stake, like all the youngsters of the same generation. As allied forces, the Soviet Union and the United States of America in those days shared the same plight. We knew that the German propaganda of the time, which aimed almost exclusively at the Russians and bolshevism, was a lie. We could not believe what we were told and we did not want to.

You, Americans, have often been surprised to see what fascination communism has exerted in Western Europe in the last forty years. But the Communists also fought with us and for us. We had to learn to listen to the faint whisper of Soviet dissidents and dissenters. We had to experience what our brothers and sisters felt in Hungary, in Czechoslovakia, and, more recently, in Poland when they stood up for their human rights and were crushed without mercy. I could also mention all the other countries throughout the world where totalitarianism brutally exposes its ugly features. But we needed to discover that the Gulag existed and that all the wonderful speech about human rights could not be trusted and could mean the exact opposite of what it claimed, before we lost our illusions, although we still instinctively subscribe to the universal power of rational and democratic ideals.

This should not give you, our American friends, any reason for political satisfaction, nor any justification for ideological righteousness. Because we all have to pay for what communism really is and for its decline. We have to ask new questions: Why has the world been shared between the allied forces at the end of the Second World War? Why did we have to cooperate with Stalin in order to overthrow Hitler? What can we say now to our brothers and sisters behind the iron curtain?

Perhaps you guess what many Europeans feel. They do not know whether the defense of human rights, as the justification of a policy, is much more than a pretext, or a hoax, or a big lie. Such a suspicion spreads all around the world, in the developing countries which struggle for economic survival and in the old Eastern civilizations which now have to assimilate our culture and our technology. If you glance at a map of the earth, you can hear the noise of collapsing ideals. What is right and what is wrong?

The most serious and deadly threat for human rights and for all that allows us to live is this: our inability to say where human rights are rationally rooted, all the while believing that they must be rooted in human reason. The problem may be that our culture is torn between two conceptions of reason. And the gap between these two visions may account for the dilemma with which we are confronted.

Nowadays one model seems to be dominant: that of technology, which does not follow any other norm than that of its own development, just as a computerized system can be developed indefinitely. Along such a line, there is no other standard than the technical feasibility within the wide range of the mathematical possibilities through which the system can express its pregnancy and power. The only question is one of consistency, costs, and profits. As soon as something becomes possible, it must be achieved, because an internal logic demands such a development and strongly objects to any moral consideration on the consequences of such development. This logic views such moral reflections as foreign and irrelevant. It is actually the case with various biological experiments and all that can now be done with the human body. It is also the case with the economy and the organization of our societies.

Moreover, it is the same with human consciousness. The triumph of technological reason is to reduce human consciousness to measurable opinions. How far we are from the distinction which the ancient philosophers established between uncertain, particular opinions, and certain, universal reason! Today what is called public opinion, what a majority (or an active minority) thinks or answers to one question, is to be welcome as the supreme and ultimate norm of what technological rationality has the right to achieve. But it is clear that measures, samples, figures, and the questions themselves that are asked are nothing but the by-products of this technological rationality. We have refused Goebbels's propaganda and Leninist methods to trigger political and social unrest. So why do we surrender so easily to the modern specialists of publicity, marketing, and the mass media?

Unfortunately, the only criticism comes from moralizing leagues of virtue, which focus narrowly on one square inch of human flesh and seem to ignore the real issue: What is public opinion? What are its rights over against reason? Can technological rationality be allowed to colonize public opinion into its system? Modern scientists know that the mere observation of a phenomenon is not without influence on it. It must be added that technological rationality simply ignores human rights. It cannot integrate such a notion. It does acknowledge its existence, because of its measurable weight in human consciousness. Human rights are then reduced to what public opinion is aware of at the moment. Europe used to be torn apart by religious wars. We then discovered that the principle *cujus regio, ejus religio,* which identified the nation and the religion of its government, and laboriously put an end to the fanaticism of the sixteenth and seventeenth centuries, was absurd after all. And the age of "Enlightenment" was praised for overwhelming the old religious fanaticism and promoting universal reason as the root of invincible human rights. But today's triumph of public opinion spells a return to the blindest and most cruelly absurd fanaticism. The best evidence for such a regression is war. Never before had there been more deaths and casualties of all kinds. Technological rationality is responsible for it.

At the same time the other form of rationality seems to be hopelessly discredited: it is philosophical or metaphysical. You may remember what Shakespeare wrote in *Macbeth:*

It is a tale
told by an idiot, full of sound and fury,
signifying nothing.

Is this the ultimate truth about humankind and the world we live in? Or is there a wisdom that does not merely consist of recipes for individual survival after the impending apocalypse? Is there a human wisdom that all can trust in and that might make our lives meaningful? Who or what can tell us that both our rights and duties are legitimate? In other words, can men and women believe that humanity, *their* humanity, is more than an abstract and empty notion which no one can take seriously? Is it possible to think of human existence as something else than a struggle for life, or the meaningless succession of generations? Is there a common good that is common to all? Does the word *humanity* still make sense?

If we answer *no,* then does our civilization have any future left? I do not mean that humankind is not the master of its future. This has become commonplace. Nor am I saying that futurology is a very uncertain science. But if we cannot say what it means to be human, then human history is strictly and literally a nonsense and this world is ruled by morons or madmen. Shakespeare did not claim to tell the whole and ultimate truth when he wrote that all was "sound and fury." We sometimes happen to experience no more; it is a fact. But is this all we can reasonably say and teach?

Let me ask you just one question: What do you think Thomas Jefferson would have answered if somebody had opposed the quotation from Shakespeare to the rational principles on which your democracy was being built? What would Jefferson say if he could participate in the debates in Congress today? Where is the philosophical optimism which fostered the ideal of human rights? This is not only *your* problem and privilege, since such an ideal characterizes our Western civilization as a whole and even the whole earth, inasmuch as it is now one world and nothing in it remains unknown thanks to technological progress.

Here is the crucial question everywhere today: What does it mean to be human? Which rationality can establish universal human rights? I went as far as I could, I repeat not as a theoretician, but as empirically as possible. Because the person in the street does not see things otherwise and knows that she is being abused. Because the average man or woman does not care about abstract principles until he or she has to face the consequences. I am now going to try to answer even more modestly the questions I have humbly asked. Allow me to make five simple points.

One. Our first duty is to acknowledge the value of what I called philosophical reason, or the philosophical exercise of reason. I know that technical rationality is founded on the positivist assumption. I also know that philosophical and theological disputes cannot be resolved in a unanimous conclusion and that, on the other hand, scientific rationality imposes limits to human certainty, therefore narrowing the field of universal agreement. Standing out for philosophical reason when technical rationality is triumphant may sound like advocating a step backward. But our recent experiences have proved that, on the contrary, this is a necessity and we must think it all over if we do not want everything to collapse in a cataclysm whose dimensions and consequences we can hardly imagine. Our reason must make new progress in order to become aware of itself and find out its universal relevance, especially in all the key areas where technical rationality ignores it or deliberately crushes it.

Is this mere wishful thinking? You may feel like replying: instead of asserting the necessity for a renewal of philosophical reason as the indispensable basis for a consistent and universal approach of humanity, its characteristics and its rights, why don't you set to work? Why don't you write or tell us *now* what we need? I simply say that this is the new frontier for human reason. The ancient Greeks had conquered this territory and we have received the heritage. Others in Asia had also explored it with their own ways and means. But haven't we finally abandoned this land which used to be ours? In the field of rationality we may have behaved like predators who leave behind them what they have consumed and destroy what they have used. It is as if the land our ancestors had conquered had no more riches to offer and we had to go somewhere else. But the motherland of reason is our root, our heritage, the womb from which everything was born. If you compare universal reason to an economic enterprise, technological rationality is like one branch of business which monopolizes all energies and investments, until the original capital is swallowed up and the company eventually goes bankrupt at the height of its commercial growth.

Since the renewal of philosophical reason has become indispensable to the survival of our civilization, I think I can assert that some men and women will acknowledge that a philosophical use of reason must not only be tolerated, but even become a priority. When I visited Berkeley in 1969, I was surprised to see how many intellectuals there at that time were interested in Eastern mysticism and wisdom. I do not see why the most advanced scientific communities today could not rediscover the roots of Western thought.

Two. If such an adventure is to take place, we must first try to understand why and how human reason has come to ignore its roots and has gone astray. This is a demand which is both intellectual and spiritual. It amounts to following in intellectual matters the advice which Saint Ignatius of Loyola gives at the end of the first week of his Exercises to the person who wishes to examine his or her spiritual journey. We can read this, in the fifth addition (77, 1): "I shall see, he said, what happened to me during the time devoted to contemplation or meditation. If it is bad, I shall look for the cause, and when I find it, I shall amend and try not to make the same mistake again. If it is good, I shall thank God our Lord and promise to do it again."

If I quote Saint Ignatius's advice concerning spirituality in the field of rationality, there is a reason. Those among you who are familiar with the Spiritual Exercises will remember that this suggestion comes at the moment when Saint Ignatius wants the disciple to remember, in a real *anamnesis*, not only his personal life but also the history of humankind as a whole. The disciple's life is part of this history and humankind is, as it were, wounded by sin and called to repentance and conversion.

Three. Consequently, such an intellectual *anamnesis* leads to identifying the shortcomings of reason as a spiritual problem. In other words, the limits which human reason imposed upon itself are to be called by their name: they are sins. This means that human reason cannot be separated from human freedom and responsibility. We probably made a mistake when we took it for granted that logical speech was no more than a pure formalism and had nothing to do with the subject who produces and uses it. We tend to confuse human reason with one of its products, for example, a computer. It is correct to say that a computer is not responsible for anything, because it is not a subject. But when a human being uses his or her reason, it is always that of a human subject who is in relation with other human subjects. Ultimately consistency or inconsistency do not decide what is right and what is wrong. What is decisive is not the means but the end which is proposed to the reasoning subject and the way he or she faces the consequences of his or her choice. Reason itself is not above the judgment of moral consciousness.

That is why it is often difficult to draw the line between philosophy and religion: human reason may well have sinned; this sin may well account for the mistake it made; this sin was a mistake, or this mistake was a sin. The link becomes evident if we remember the Nazi atrocities which I have already mentioned. But we might just as easily become responsible for other abominations through various human endeavors which offer tempting self-justifications.

Just one example: slavery. How could we today account for it in the name of universal reason? But the economic rationality justified it for three centuries in Christian nations. Nowadays many of your fellow citizens, whose ancestors were captured and deported to this free land, still bear the consequences of such an aberration. Let us not forget that perhaps as many as sixty million Africans were sent as slaves to the Americas. I know that it was in the United States that people fought and died to win the emancipation of black Americans. And *you* know what price your country had to pay for this and how much this still costs. Was this a mere temporary shortcoming of reason? I must call it a sin, even as I remember that we Europeans were by no means innocent.

Four. This leads us to the point that human reason can also be redeemed. The early Christian theologians coined a formula which caused many controversies because it is provocative and paradoxical: *Spoliatus in gratuitis: vulneratus in naturalibus*. The human being is spoiled of, that is, robbed of, what God had graciously given him: the joy of a divinization for no other reason than love. And humankind is also wounded in what makes up human nature. Of course this is to be understood quite realistically and historically. The biblical, Christian and Catholic tradition takes into account the concrete and empirical human condition. All is rooted in the history of the People of God, in the historical circumstances in which God spoke to Israel, and in which today Christians recognize Jesus as the Messiah and the Word of God made flesh. The absolute is given to humans at the level of their historical experience. It provides a universal approach of the singularity of each person. This universality is that of love. When Jesus is asked who or what humans are, he answers: your neighbor. This means that the universal and redeeming rationality is to be experienced as forgiveness, mercy, hope, brotherhood, and love. What else can bring humans together while respecting the individuality of each? What else can they have in common?

But we know that humans are not always capable of loving one another and accepting such a logic, although it is the only universal one. Experience teaches us all that the human reason in which human dignity is rooted is sick and wounded. If it is to work again, it must be healed and not simply repaired. Reason is not something purely mechanical. The reasoning subject is ignored when it is reduced to a combination of wheels. If human reason must be redeemed, it is because it is that of a subject who is wounded and has to be healed. A person cannot be healed in the same way a machine can (or cannot) be repaired. If something goes wrong and there is a terrible accident, it will not be enough to rebuild the machine and check all the stages of the process. Such a procedure presupposes that humans master the tools they create and that the problem is merely technical.

But when human reason errs and sins, human beings do not face tools they have created. They face another subject on whom they depend, that is to say, God himself. However, it would be a fatal mistake to consider humans as products manufactured by God. God does not make humans like they design and use tools. But God creates us as subjects, as free persons to his image and likeness. This is why the key word in the Gospel is "conversion." Humans are called to turn to God, as subjects using their reason in a personal relationship.

Five. I now reach the last point I wish to make. There remains one question: Can and should the Church claim a role in the establishment and defense of human rights? The answer is *yes.* Christianity has indeed played a decisive part throughout history in the awakening of human consciousness. But this is not exclusively Christian. After all, many atheists or agnostics or nonbelievers are entitled to think that there is no reason why Christians in general and more especially Catholics should claim as their privilege what is universal. They may find in such claims some perverse kind of imperialism and intolerance. This seems to be the case in most current ethical debates: all that Christians say often sounds like a limitation imposed upon the others' freedom. The reason for such a misunderstanding is apparently that most people actually believe, at least implicitly, that anybody can do anything, that this is what freedom means and that the very idea of a universal norm would amount to a negation of human rights. If reason gives up its universal dimension, misgivings are bound to become unavoidable.

But the role of Christians and Catholics is not to impose anything upon others: through their own conversion they are to cooperate with the work of salvation, they are to become the messengers of the Good News. Their mission is to make Christ present, to introduce him, here and now, among the men and women with whom they have become brothers and sisters, thanks to divine grace and gifts. The sacraments of the Church, which make up its heart, are the means for the salvation of humans and their reason, so that human reason can be healed and recover its dignity, so that every human being, whether or not he or she be Christian, can already benefit from this recovery of a universal rationality.

The Second Vatican Council solemnly reasserted the fundamental and absolute dignity of the human person. This is especially clear in the Declaration on Religious Freedom to which the American bishops and theologians contributed decisively. Contrary to what some critics hinted, this was not sinking into some kind of relativism or indifferentism. It rather means that the unconditional dignity of every single human being is already a fruit of Christ's redemption. The birth of the new Adam, in the person of the resurrected Son of God, allows human reason to recognize universal human rights. The particular story of Jesus the Christ has introduced a universal dimension in human history and healed the wounds of human reason. Because Christ gave to reason a universal relevance, every human being can claim for himself or herself the same rights as any other and acknowledge that he or she has the same duties. Christ's glory restores and reveals human dignity.

POLAND

Christianity's Hidden Resources

Your Excellency, you were appointed bishop of Orleans and then archbishop of Paris by John Paul II. Last year the pope visited France. Could I ask you what the present pope means to the Church in France and to you personally?

I would rather speak for myself than for the Church in France. I will tell you what I was thinking and saying long before the pope hauled me out to set me in my present place. My first impression at the pope's election was of unbelievable joy and great hope. I thought the Lord had a wonderful sense of humor. There was the relation between John Paul I and John Paul II. I consider that the brief pontificate of John Paul I had an unusual logic about it. God sent him only so that John Paul II could succeed him; that's one way of looking at the meaning of events. To my mind the pontificate of John Paul I was one of the greatest, since it was because of him that it became possible to point the Church in a new direction.

Second, I will now say what I thought at the time of the election of John Paul II without knowing that I would one day be able to tell it to the Poles. It seemed to me at the time as if God were being incredibly logical. It all took place as if a whole area of strength for Christianity, which had until then remained obscured, came into the light. In fact it was a whole part of the history of the Church which had remained hidden to the West and which turned out to be in reserve. It was the same with the special destiny of the Polish nation; it symbolized that hidden face of the Church. What happened was that someone who, from the Western point of view, seemed like a stranger in the eyes of the multitude was put at the head of the Church. It was rather like David who, from minding his sheep, became the anointed of the Lord.

I am a great friend of the Vietnamese who live here in France. One of them

An interview with Jerzy Turowicz, published in *Tygodnik Powszechny*, 23 March 1981, reprinted in the *Osservatore Romano*, French edition, 6 October 1981.

told me that, when he heard of the election of John Paul II, he wept with joy. When I asked why, he answered "Because he will understand us." I said, "Why especially him? He has never been to Vietnam." "Never mind," he answered, "he knows what it is to belong to a nation which has been severely tried; so he will understand us."

To put it another way, I think that the choice of such a pope is something of absolutely decisive significance for the history of the Church. It is the first time that a pope has lived through the crisis of our times personally and in his own homeland. I am thinking of those terrifying upheavals which have affected humankind, and also of the way in which they have been caused by a modern phenomenon, the rationalism which would like to dominate history and society, but which often becomes the source of cruelty instead. All this means that what seemed the greatest hope can become the greatest setback and lead to the utmost suffering.

This is a pope who lived through the last war and who experienced in his own person all the terrible traumas of his country which went through so much. He has lived through the crises of the last fifty years. His own formation took place in the midst of philosophical controversy with atheism and a critique of the atheistic systems of thought which now claim a large part of humanity. At the same time the pope shared the life of a Church composed of ordinary people which, in spite of its weaknesses and its sins, found its sources of strength as it went through great trials. That is the grace which has been given to the Church. It is as if the Lord were saying to us Westerners, tired and jaded as we are, "I have for you hidden resources." I would see this as the coming of a true modernism, rather as if someone from modern Europe were succeeding someone from ancient Rome. In that sense, I think that Pope John Paul II is the most modern pope we have ever had.

I find in myself a deep bond, at both the intuitive and the intellectual level, with the way in which John Paul II expresses his ideas and his position.

Another thing which is startling and very wonderful is his way of governing the Church. His pontificate has been noted for the way he has innovated and gone forward; in my view he has taken great steps forward, and you can see that if you look at the situation of the Church. Sometimes I hear people saying that they do not know what the pope is thinking; people say that. In fact nearly everybody is saying it, but I do not agree. I think that it is perfectly obvious what the pope is thinking. One only has to listen to what he is saying. His deep cunning consists in saying what he really thinks; I suppose that is the deepest cunning.

By traveling the pope unites the churches and makes them become aware of themselves. He is a real successor of Saint Peter, bishop of Rome. In the way he presents himself he has found an ideal formula which has enormous ecumenical significance. He arrives, visits the churches, and urges them to unite as if he wanted to bring them a mirror in which they could see themselves as churches of the one Catholic Church. This apostolic ministry, combined with the Roman centralization which remains the instrument of government, is like the new reality which was announced by Vatican II, synodal government.

Can you remember what the press was saying in France and in America before the election of John Paul II? Do you remember their description of contemporary Catholicism and how they saw the role of the pope? Did you see the petition of the American theologians and the articles in the French press and elsewhere? Anyway, people were saying that the papal ministry was exhausted, that the Church had to give up everything in order to survive. I don't know how to put it; there was a feeling of weariness and of resignation. And then this pope comes along, full of energy, and the exact opposite happens. It is obvious that one's personal gifts, one's charisma, have a lot to do with it, but I would say that these gifts, this charisma, come along at the time that God wanted, precisely when they were most needed. If it had not been Karol Wojtyla, it would have been someone like him because the time was right; it just had to be someone like that.

In that sense the coming of this pope is something decisive. Providence would have given us a pope of that type in any case. It is the grace that we need today.

In the early days of the present pope's reign, I used to have a quiet chuckle to myself. There was something to laugh about every time news came. The impression I had was that he was doing things with ruthless logic and that he was being very wily, although *wily* is not quite the right word. He knew perfectly well what the difficulties were and he had great courage in facing up to them. He had great wisdom and it wasn't the wisdom of Don Quixote tilting at windmills, but the wisdom of God which can measure the obstacles and thus overcome them. The pope is thus able to smooth out the way and many facts indicate this. My impression is that an important page has been turned in the history of the Church. The Church is really ceasing to be only a Western Church and, thanks to this pope, its modern character is becoming truly evident. But he also has a really deep sense of history and of historical continuity, and so his vision is intensely traditional. That is precisely what the Church needs today, an authentic sense of historical continuity and of the scope of unfolding history. Such a pope was necessary in all probability so that the Eastern dimension of the Church could become apparent; I mean Eastern in relation to the Oder-Neisse Line.[1] It is an important moment for us Westerners; it is a moment of grace.

Your Excellency, can I ask you another question? You have been speaking about John Paul II, about Poland and its place in the Church together with Eastern

---

1. The Oder-Neisse Line is the border between East Germany and Poland since 1945. (Translator's note)

Europe. You have mentioned what that part of Europe can give to the Church. But what does Poland mean to you, whose parents were Polish Jews? Could you tell us whether you have a personal relation with Poland?

Well, it's all rather symbolic; it's a part of my memories and of my "memories of memories." The fact is that I remember my parents' reminiscences; that's why I call them "memories of memories." However, there is a certain similarity in the way one feels about things; I can't quite define it. It is true that I am French and that France is my homeland; and yet I must admit that I have these "memories of memories." They do not constitute nostalgia but they are tenuous impressions. For instance, although this may seem childish, I know what *barszez*[2] is because we used to eat it at home, even though my mother was killed during the German occupation of France. There are a lot of little things like that. There are other things which are difficult to evaluate but more important, things linked to Polish culture; even when they are not, it means that I feel a certain affinity with it. All this became more conscious when I got to know something of the history of the Polish people and discovered that our roots were closely intertwined over several centuries.

One feels these things, although one cannot always call them to conscious memory; it is something that one carries inside oneself like a precious secret. One cannot express these things adequately. It is difficult to express all this side of oneself to do with feelings; I have already mentioned the reaction of the Vietnamese when the pope was elected; I think the dramatic side of Polish history provides a good basis for understanding all the situations of our modern world: it is the history of a country which has been repeatedly stripped of its identity; its very existence as a nation has been denied; its frontiers have been so often moved backwards and forwards; its political and national identity have been so often trampled on.

Throughout the world there are so many immigrants and many of these are Polish immigrants. I think that within Poland those who have been moved from one part of the country to another outnumber the rest. Centuries of experience of being moved from place to place afford the possibility of understanding what is happening throughout the world and of understanding the tragedy and the hopes of humanity.

I come back to what I have said about the pope because it is something which affects me and corresponds to my own experience. When you see him and listen to him you can sense behind his words the fundamental optimism of the faith. It is not a naive optimism but one which is conversant with the tragic experience of human life. This is something really Christian, it seems to me. This is what gives to Christian hope the strength of its conviction, because that hope is not a fairy story. It is not a hope which gives a false or unreal comfort; it has a strength which can face the greatest fear.

2. *Barszez* is a Polish dish, a soup made with red beetroot. (Translator's note)

If hope were something taking our attention away from life and focusing it on dreams, then there would be the danger of alienation. But if, on the contrary, hope enables us to face the very worst, then it becomes instantly stronger than the worst reality. This is the special characteristic of Christian hope. That is why it is not an illusion.

I find myself in what the pope says, although our worlds are so very different. He has a deeply realistic way of speaking, which recognizes human-kind in its true situation and gives him ways of experiencing the hope which comes from God together with the strength which God gives it. That is not the language of dreams or of sleep. It is a more realistic way of speaking than what is normally called realistic because it can encompass everything, includ-ing all those ideological ways of speaking with their deadly results. So the pope's way of speaking brings about an encounter between the victim and its oppressor; what happens is that not only does the victim express its own suffering but it also explains the condition of the oppressor. When that happens, when the victim can explain not only its own condition but also that of its oppressor, then the victim becomes the ultimate truth for the oppressor too. That seems to me very important today in view of the historical situation we are in.

Prayer for Gdansk

Since the news has come through about the military coup which is crushing Poland, the same question is being asked repeatedly: "What can we do?" For Christians the question is more searching; we are asking: "Does the Polish hierarchy preach submission with the same compromise in view as Western diplomats, a compromise which you can call realistic, cowardly, or just resigned? Can't Christians say anything apart from advocating escape into spiritual considerations? Isn't there more than praying that we can do? Isn't the Church coming to terms with the big battalions once more through what John Paul II and Archbishop Glemp have said?" This is a case where good intentions are not enough to understand the position which they are taking up; it is a position which is realistic politically but, more important, it is unavoidable spiritually.

May I first of all recall something obvious; if Poles today are faced with despair, their despair did not begin recently. It goes back to 1939. At that time the other European nations did not want to lose lives over Danzig; since then Poland has lost six million lives. The carving up of the world which followed Yalta has meant that Poland has lost the possibility of a democratic existence. Now the Solidarity movement which was based exclusively on legal rights has been opposed by brute force; so there is no possibility of any political solution in Poland. Inside the country, the situation is blocked by martial law; outside the country, it is blocked by the division of Europe into two camps which the West certainly cannot modify and does not want to modify.

Such a deadlock would, humanly speaking, lead to despair. Despair leads to death, whether it be death by an armed uprising bloodily suppressed or death by normal police methods or death by individual suicides. You cannot share things with a devouring fire. If today Poles are once again prepared to

An article in *Le Monde*, 18 December 1981.

die for Poland, then Poland will die. Their national anthem says: "Poland will not die as long as we live," but if all Poles die, Poland will die. The alternative is not freedom or death (because an uprising to fight for freedom would mean certain death) but death or life.

But what sort of life would it be? Isn't life without freedom something subhuman? First of all, may I point out that we, who are well-off and who think only of our cowardly ease, are not well placed to give others a lesson in heroism. I also note that all the political analyses of the situation (including my own) fall very far short of the reality. If Poland has not disappeared since 1939 and especially in the last six months, it is because its *spiritual* life has kept it going. In Poland a whole nation has experienced what Solzhenitsyn and others experienced as individuals; I mean the power of the Spirit, the strength of an authentic morality, the salvation given by God in death itself. All this has been lived by the Poles with Solidarity and around the Black Virgin of Czestochowa.

Lech Walesa once said to me: "I have no weapons but truth, faith, and prayer. I have nothing to lose except my own life and I give that freely." He was saying something which is obvious, both to himself and to us. What has given the Poles a slightly better deal within the totalitarian camp is their spiritual strength; with it went their just demands but, if they had existed on their own, these demands would not even have been expressed openly.

Today only that spiritual strength can allow the Poles to overcome a trial which is humanly speaking unbearable. The temptation today is suicide; the use of force is doomed in advance and it would destroy the future. The duty of Poles today is not to draw the sword from the scabbard, as Christ told Saint Peter (Matt. 26:52 and parallels). It means accepting to tolerate the intolerable; in Christian terms, it means accepting the Passion.

The passion of Poland today is having the spiritual courage to live and not to die, not to commit suicide by turning to violence. It is a duty to survive so as to outlive violence, as Archbishop Glemp proclaimed: "The Church will not compromise in relation to human life. It does not matter if the Church is accused of cowardice . . . the Church wants to defend each human life; therefore in this present state of martial law, the Church calls for peace whenever possible; it calls for an end to violence and for the avoidance of any fighting between brothers, should it break out."

When one is faced with violence, the only response, if one wants to live, is the refusal of violence. That is the exact opposite, in spiritual and political terms, of the pacifist saying: "Better red than dead," because what is asked of the Poles is not to connive at injustice but to triumph over it by the strength of unarmed innocence. The victim must outlive the oppressor.

That is why prayer is the *first* duty. We must ask God that the Polish people, which has survived by means of its spiritual strength in the past and which has achieved a minimum of solidarity by its spiritual power, may find enough spiritual resources now to bear the unbearable. May it not hurl itself into collective suicide by a resource to violence which is politically without solution.

We must pray too so that we can come to realize that it is the Poles who are paying the price of the peace which we enjoy. More than thirty years ago we paid for that peace, not with thirty pieces of silver but with their enslavement. We should pray that we may come to realize that they are far ahead of us in terms of spiritual strength; in a sense we have nothing great enough or strong enough to give to them. We should pray for understanding, that we may come to accepting something else that Walesa once told me: "I cannot understand you Westerners. You have everything and yet you lack all reason for living. We have nothing but we know what life is for and this is what makes us happy." In fact Poland is giving us much more than we can give to Poland. It has demonstrated what spiritual power can achieve, both politically and socially.

That is why we must hope (and in Christian terms that means pray) that Poland can give us still more. May it show us that its strength enables it to live through an unlivable situation and to survive in spite of all the various forms of death invented by human beings. We must dare to believe in the power of peace; dare to believe in love which is stronger than death; dare to believe that Christ can give us resurrection.

All this can only be taught to us, who are rich but with hearts of stone, by those who are poor and empty-handed. They are the ones God loves first because they bear, more than anyone, his image and likeness.

Their Struggle Is Ours

2 Sam. 7:1–16
Rom. 16:25–27
Luke 1:26–38

W hat we are doing this evening is fulfilling a promise. When I saw Lech Walesa and Archbishop Glemp, the primate of Poland, they already knew that somehow, someday, the test would come as it had done so often in the past. They made me promise: "When it comes, you will pray *with* us," not only *for* us. If we are praying today, it is so that we can be with them. That is a sufficient answer, as far as the believer is concerned, to the question: "What is the use of praying?" We are praying because they asked us to, because we promised them that we would, and because prayer enables us to experience the very same faith, truth, and fidelity which are keeping them alive at this moment.

The words of the Gospel which we have just heard this evening take on a new and surprising meaning. We heard the words: "Everything is possible to God" and "Behold the handmaid of the Lord; be it done to me according to your word"; as we did so, we remembered those other words of Christ at the agony in the Garden, just before the Passion, "Father, everything is possible to you. Take this cup away from me. Yet not what I will but what you will."

So are we faced with the Nativity or the Passion, with birth or with death, with hope or with the entry into the mystery of the cross? What we are called upon to do tonight is to understand that there are two sides of the one mystery; we are experiencing it here and they are experiencing it over there. These two situations, although they are very different from each other, throw light on each other.

I have just read the Gospel of the Annunciation. Our brothers in Poland

A sermon preached at the Cathedral of Notre-Dame de Paris, 19 December 1981.

are hearing the same words in all the churches this evening. And yet I have alluded to the agony of Christ. Just think what that word means. It does not mean the last moment of a dying person: *agony* means *contest*. The Gospel uses that word to describe the prayer of Christ. So we have to try to understand what that contest is. The Poles are living through it; we can share in it and it finds its origin in the struggle of Christ during his prayer as he prepares to enter into his Passion. Their struggle has been plunging us into distress for the last eight days, but perhaps we have not understood exactly what it consists of. Nor have we understood those who have been able to speak about this struggle, the primate and the bishops of Poland. They have vindicated in the clearest and most disinterested way the right to justice, freedom, and truth; and at the same time they have asked, as John Paul II himself has done, that lives should be spared and they have prayed that blood may not be shed once again. And yet we have not understood all this.

What then is the situation of our brothers and sisters over there? Why have they asked us to pray for them tonight? It is a situation where they can expect no help apart from their own resources. It is a situation where they know they are alone. In that situation their faith consists in those very words we have just heard, "Everything is possible to God." Their only weapon against power and violence consists in the omnipotence of faith in God, because God cannot allow the disappearance of what constitutes humanity's deepest reasons for living. The strength of that faith is unconquerable and cannot be suppressed because it is the faith of men and women who receive from God their dignity and their liberty; they thus receive the strength to resist what would be their spiritual annihilation, even to the point of giving up life itself. In their state of utter weakness, their act of faith consists in opposing force and compulsion only by placing their own weakness in the hands of God.

Thus the measure of a person is revealed when he or she surrenders to something greater. The measure of a person's dignity is to be in the image and likeness of God. Those who have the courage to believe that cannot be overcome. But if the Poles are prepared to live out that faith, then they come face to face with the threat of death and with actual death, just like the Suffering Servant of the Bible.

How can hope be strong enough to keep the door of faith open when there is no help at hand? How can it maintain dignity and the will to fight? How can one have the audacity to oppose violence with the sole weapons of peace and love? How can one fight injustice with justice only and oppression with freedom? For the disciples of Christ the hour of spiritual conflict consists of decisions like these; it is an hour of conflict which is lived with Christ. Our brothers and sisters have entered into the hour of their temptation.

What is the nature of their temptation? Those of you who know the Gospels will remember that all those who were with Jesus in his Passion were tempted. First of all, there was the temptation of falling prey to *sleep*. That means the annihilation of oneself, submission, accepting to lose one's dignity and one's conscience.

Then there is the temptation to *suicide*. Remember that Judas after the Passion of Christ gave way to despair and killed himself. In a way, death can mesmerize us as a means of getting out of being dishonored. But such despair is a refusal of faith. We must pray that they fall not into such temptation.

Then there is the temptation of *running away*. The apostles did that; they fled. They abandoned the reasons which give meaning to life in order to save their life.

In their isolation, our brothers and sisters in Poland are facing death and they are being subjected to the same temptations. Their prayer is like that of Mary, united to Christ in his Passion, in a situation of utter weakness. We are praying tonight so that we can bear with them the same trial and the same struggle. They will live by their faith. By it they will receive life, but it will be at the cost of submitting to the Passion. By their faith they will show forth the power of a love disarmed, facing all those regimes which deny human dignity or repress human freedom.

What about us? What can we do? Our situation is very different, so are our possibilities. Our first duty, hoping that the news will get through and that they will know about it, is to show that we are their brothers and sisters, able to share their suffering, and to tell them that we love them, respect them, and believe in them.

Then we have the duty of praying, we who are believers and disciples of Christ, so that we can share in their struggle. We have to enter into the same contest they are in, facing violence with love as their only weapon. If we want to do that, then we must count the cost. Only those who have never experienced such a struggle can think that it is a matter of words only. But, if we enter into the struggle, we too will be faced with the same temptations.

The temptation of *sleep* will be for us the danger of forgetting it all, once the emotion dies down. We will run the risk of going to sleep by forgetting the fate which has overtaken our brothers and sisters, as we have done after the disappearance of the freedom of so many nations.

Our second temptation will be *suicide,* being attracted by death. That means despairing of the possibility of justice, truth, the power of freedom, and human dignity. We have done that on previous occasions. We have accepted things as they are, as if nothing could be done about it except submit to fate. That is a kind of suicide because it means the loss of our dignity.

Our third temptation is *betrayal* or *flight*, like the apostles. We would be doing that if we used the same weapons as the people we are fighting, instead of relying on the truth of love. To betray and take flight means to fight hatred with hatred, aggression with aggression, wrong with wrong, and murder with murder. To be unfaithful to the reasons we have, or should have, for living, that is betrayal. To give up freedom in order to save freedom, that would be betrayal: so would giving up human dignity in order to save it or abandoning the truth to save the truth.

So you see that we, the people of the West, reared as we are by Christianity, cannot avoid facing in our situation the same spiritual trial as the people of Poland, but in different circumstances. You who are Christians must know that you will need the same courage and faith to face that threefold temptation in the fight which is ours. We need the same faith and love over here, so that men and women can dare to believe that it is not inevitable that humankind would be enslaved by its own or that human dignity should be denied by one who should be a brother or sister. We are going to need as much love and faith as they do to ensure that the voice of the just man crying to heaven does not fall silent. We shall need the same faith in the power of God so that we can dare to hope and not to become resigned.

May I end with a quotation from Solzhenitsyn: "in general, no one has the right to require others to make a sacrifice; one can invite to it, but only on condition that one first shows how it should be done" *(The Oak and the Calf)*.

EUROPE

Europe's Spiritual Future

Who are we, Europeans? What are the frontiers of our space? How can one draw the boundaries of today's Europe, which is still called Western, so that it indicates who belongs to Europe to the north, to the south, and to the east? How can we find our own identity, since the history of our European nations has been reproduced in the New World since the sixteenth century beyond the Western promontories of our continent? And what about the various conflicting offshoots of our culture in Africa and Asia?

Who are we? What are the limits of our memory? Who can draw up the list of what is lawfully our inheritance? Is it enough to claim descent from Greece and Rome and the dual empire, Byzantine and Latin on the one hand; and on the other to trace our descent from Israel and the Church of Jesus Christ, a Church divided successively between East and West, north and south? How much can the Europe of today receive the contribution of the many rich national cultures of Europe, which have often been ignored or forgotten, and some of which have disappeared? Who are we, Europeans? What is our future? In asking such questions, am I initially giving too much place to nostalgia and to the fears which are present in even the highest and most clear-sighted of European consciences?

There is after all an evil spirit which broods over Europe and its past. It is the guilt which comes from achieving brilliant success at the cost of the very principles which have made such a success possible. Thus the proclamation of freedom became the will to dominate. The pursuit of equality produced slavery. The affirmation of brotherhood became the origin of countless bloody struggles and of hopeless divisions. That is why our future bears the

An address given at Bonn to the German hierarchy, the government, members of the Bundestag, and the diplomatic corps, 8 October 1981.

burden of self-doubt which caused, at the time when we were young, the deadly quarrels of war.

It is not for me to guess what the economic or political situation will be in the future. What I have to do in the sight of God is to look at our times from the spiritual point of view so that we can face up to our guilty conscience and explore to the full the ordeal caused by suspicion.

Historically Europe's fate has been to dominate other nations until eventually it became branded by the term *domination*. From the Atlantic to the Urals the struggle caused by domination and slavery has come to divide Europe itself. What it imposed on others has become its own fate or, as Paul would say, it has become "God's anger" on Europe (cf. Rom. 1:18). The domination of those who were masters and the violence shown to those who were slaves were Europe's crime and its shame, before they furnished an ideology for those who proclaimed a master race. Blood was spilt in all the countries of Europe; regimes, parties, and states came to an end in bloody combat. The lust for mastery and bitter violence still flourish. Even today there are nations in Europe suffering under the ideology of domination which Europe itself has produced. I pay tribute to these people today, to their resistance and to their solidarity.

Thanks to Europe, the revolt of slaves became the experience of other parts of the world. Then it became the fate of Europe itself and tormented it, before becoming a class ideology. May all the sorrows engendered by these struggles bring to an end the regimes, parties, and states which are based on slavery and still batten on servitude. I make an appeal to those European people who might be tempted by these slave regimes; I appeal to their clear-sightedness and to their vigilance.

Two world wars have had their beginnings in Europe, a Europe divided by its destiny of becoming a master fallen into slavery. The divisions of Europe, which have been the legacy of these wars, have compromised Europe's future, though they have not prevented it from becoming wealthy. East and West are now locked in deadly combat. But we are not the only ones who impose the cost of our wars and of our weapons on the people in the world who are dying of hunger. Thus Europe, both free Europe and Europe in chains, has wanted to become wealthy and has made itself wealthy at the expense of those who are the poorest in the world. In order to provide a base for its strength, and sometimes for its use of force, Europe has weakened so many nations and has impoverished them. It gave away its surplus, as it is still doing, but it took from the poor what they need to live. We are deaf and dumb before those who are being exploited and their cries call to heaven for vengeance.

There are apparently laws which control markets and there are economic rules. How can these laws and rules be reconciled with justice when they trace on our planet a frontier between north and south which also marks the limits of hunger? We should not be dominated by a sense of guilt; but we can only be free if we confess that we have connived in the misery of the poor. It is only right that we should do something to put a stop to it; even more so, we should not try to forget the curse which is on those who are feasting while the poor Lazarus is at the gate (Luke 16).

Europe has been under a curse as if it had shed blood. It has never ceased to shed its own blood; it is both master and slave; it is wealthy, yet its very wealth threatens it with poverty. It has shed the blood of its children in many wars; it has sought to feed them on the sweat of others. And now, as if exhausted by violence, Europe is hardly capable of transmitting life to new generations; poor, wounded Europe is causing the springs of life to run dry. The fruitfulness of love is under attack and the fruits of love are being aborted.

So the terrible problems I have mentioned, the violence of masters and slaves, the rich becoming richer and the poor becoming poorer, are being added to by the distress of those couples whose love is without life and whose life is without love. Men and women in Europe are courted by domination and seduction; they are more interested in survival than in giving to life its full potential. Couples in Europe, whether rich or poor, master or slave, are diminished by the death-dealing contradictions of their situation rather than quickened by the breath of love.

Is Europe therefore condemned to despair, as the criticisms and the denials of its young people seem to indicate? Are the men and women of our generation condemned to nostalgia for past glories, to an acknowledgment of present insoluble contradictions, and to a bad conscience for crimes whose responsibility they do not see their way to assuming? Is the youth of Europe reduced to a choice between deadly apathy and morbid violence?

We must acknowledge, however, that there are courageous people today, as there were in the past, who work unstintingly for justice and produce generous results thereby. How can one explain that these numerous and very real efforts remain hidden most of the time and never seem capable of overcoming the forces which oppose them?

Just as the demons of violence often lurk under the appearances of decency, so it is with the works of peace; they are condemned to remaining unknown and forgotten because sin prevents us from recognizing them. The good which is being achieved can never be acknowledged until the evil which was done is identified and forgiven.

Europe is not "without hope and without God in the world" (Eph. 2:12). Europe is not without a Messiah, nor is it a "stranger to the covenants of the promise" of God (Eph. 2:12). The spiritual condition of our times is not a disaster because the hope that has been given to us "does not disappoint us" (Rom. 5:5). We do not have to deny any aspect of our violence or our faults, but we, "who once were far off, have been brought near in the blood of

Christ. For he is our peace who has made us both one" (Eph. 2:13–4). We should not play down the crisis of our times, the violence, the injustice, the hatred, and the turning away from God. But all that can be atoned for; we really believe that. Everything can be reconciled; that is our hope. Love has been given to us (cf. Rom. 5:5) so that we can work at the task.

The people chosen by God are celebrating this very day the Day of the Great Atonement, Yom Kippur. What sort of repentance and expiation should Christian nations show in order to receive pardon for all the innocent people who have been slaughtered? "He was despised and rejected by men, a man of sorrows and acquainted with grief and as one from whom men hide their faces. . . . Surely he has borne our griefs, and carried our sorrows; and yet we esteemed him stricken, smitten by God and afflicted. But he was wounded for our transgressions, he was bruised for our iniquities; upon him was the chastisement that made us whole, and with his stripes we are healed" (Isa. 53:3–5). Such is the faith of Israel. It is the suffering of Israel and of its Messiah, crushed by our murderous oppositions, which atones for the sins of the world and purifies them (cf. Isa. 53:10–12). This is the faith of the People of God in its entirety. Everything had been consigned to sin (Gal. 3:22) in a common captivity, but it was the Messiah who paid the price to free us from the curse by becoming himself a curse for us (Gal. 3:13). We Christians have that faith and we have that hope; Christ Jesus, the Messiah of Israel, has by his cross, destroyed the hatred (Eph. 2:16).

Without Jesus Christ, there is no spiritual future for Europe, that Europe which was once Christian. He is the one who can still reconcile our fates by healing the wounds of old. In him, slaves or masters are no longer locked in violence (Gal. 3:28). He became poor so that by his poverty he might enrich us. In him, man and woman are not liable anymore to mutual contradiction (Gal. 3:28). Since in him there is no longer Greek or Jew (Col. 3:11) and since all have access to the same covenant with God, we can all be one in him (Gal. 3:28) as he is everything in us (Col. 3:11).

The future of Europe is not based first and foremost on its political power. It does not depend on its economic condition nor even on its cultural inheritance. Its future is uncertain if it depends on men and women who are divided by hatred. Our future lies in having hope and faith in the one who daily atones for our violence and injustice. If we belong to him by faith, then we can enter into the promises God made "to Abraham and his posterity forever" (Luke 1:55).

This promise constitutes for the Christians of Europe a vocation and a pressing duty. Through it Europe as a whole can fulfill for all the nations the hope which has sprung from it. John Paul II said this last year when he visited your country. He talked about the past relations between Germany and Poland and then said: "the building of a better future for the nations is not only a possibility; it is a serious obligation for us, our task in this second millennium after Christ which has now reached its final stage" (Speech on leaving Germany, 19 November 1980).

Speaking to the German nation, the pope launched an appeal to Europe "for a world civilization of love." He called his appeal a challenge and said that it constituted the historic answer that the future can give to the painful experiences of the past.

The pope considers that the time has come:

> Enough time has elapsed since the last war, a catastrophe which passed through Europe and through our homelands like an earthquake . . . now we are beginning to think about the future of Europe, not from a position of economic domination and selfishness but from the point of view of the civilization of love. It allows each nation to be truly itself and it frees all nations, if they are prepared to act as a community, from the threat of another conflict and of mutual destruction. It is love which allows everyone to feel truly free in the full possession of his own dignity. For that to happen there must be a policy of solidarity based on justice which will make it impossible for anyone to exploit his neighbor in his own interest. At the same time any form of abuse or oppression is ruled out. [Speech on leaving Germany, 19 November 1980]

I have come to you fully conscious of what I represent in the way of your painful past history, but I came to you in obedience to a pressing sense of duty. I just had to add my voice to this appeal addressed by the pope to the whole of Europe.

I wanted to carry in my own person and to exhibit publicly here the bad conscience of our elders, the silence of our fathers, and the rebellion of sons and daughters. Our two nations must discover again, in pardon and peace, the joy and the pride which come from a past in which love has already achieved so much in the way of civilization. I wanted to do something to change a bad conscience and the silence which comes from shame into the courage which comes from truth. It is the task of Christians, insofar as they can, to turn the confession of sin into joy and reconciliation. The frank avowal of the past, with its weaknesses and its greatness, must become a source of strength for the future. We must respond to the appeal which old Europe has received from all the continents of the world through the voice of John Paul II.

The Christian Origins of
European Culture

*I*t *looks as though the Catholic Church is favorable to the idea of Europe. But what sort of Europe?*

One needs to go back to an idea which has been forgotten recently, the idea of Central Europe. In our culture Central Europe has played an important part, although it has faded out in recent years. Kafka, Freud, Einstein, and many others were its products; our modern culture had its center somewhere between Vienna and Paris, on a line running between Berlin, Cracow, Prague, Munich, and Milan. Now we have to put on a historical exhibition in Paris to remind our intellectual classes of these things. It showed how that Europe was forced into silence and emigrated. When its remnants have survived, they have met up again in the United States or, less often, in France, England, or other Western countries. It was a culture that was steamrollered by the Communist takeover and, before that had come, by the steamroller of Nazi totalitarianism.

So that is the first task; we have to be reminded of the cultural and historical dimensions of Europe, especially of that part of it which is hidden from sight. That means Central Europe, now lost or disappeared, and Eastern Europe, including Russia which is a part of Europe's historical heritage and culture.

So you weren't surprised when Pope John Paul II used the expression "from the Atlantic to the Urals" in speaking of Europe?

Europe was and is composed of different nations, many of which had, until recent years, disappeared from view. We seem to have accepted as a fact the disappearance of Central Europe after two world wars. The conquerors of

An interview with Gwendoline Jarcyk and Henri Tincq, published in *La Croix*, 31 March 1984.

1918 created a certain sort of Europe; those of 1945 shared it out between them. In fact what we have done since is restrict the idea of Europe to the political and strategic situation of the Cold War which followed. Now there is only Western Europe and Eastern Europe; between them are the iron curtain and the Berlin Wall.

This violence and this separation have been a disaster and it seems to have caused a loss of memory in most European nations, especially in the West. Kundera[1] said recently that Central Europe has been "vampired," emptied of its content and substance by the political regimes of the Marxist-Leninist kind and by the events which followed their establishment.

How do you explain this silence about Central Europe?

I must say that it is something that I find mysterious. I belong to the generation which reached the age of twenty just after the 1939–45 war. We relied on the memories of those who had lived between the two wars but they never spoke of the time before 1939; and yet the great upheaval of the countries of Central Europe was then well underway already, partly as a result of the Treaty of Versailles. When you read the memoirs of those who knew Austria-Hungary from the beginning of the century to the eve of the Second World War, such as Manès Sperber,[2] then you can see what happened. It was the intelligentsia of the West which panicked and gave way on two occasions, at the beginnings of Leninism and at the beginnings of Nazism.

After the war was over, the same thing happened again; the intelligentsia gave way and connived at what was happening. We were told that everything was allright; France was very proud of its standing in Czechoslovakia! Nobody spoke the truth; that's all. These countries literally disappeared from the Western scene at the very time when their society was threatened and then dismantled by communism and Soviet weaponry. The eyewitnesses were too frightened to say anything. The refugees said nothing or else could not be heard.

What are the strong points of our European identity?

We need to meditate on our history and to remember the cultural inheri-

1. Milan Kundera (b. 1929) is a Czechoslovak writer who had to leave his country after the events of 1968. He writes in Czech, the English translations of his works being: *The Joke* (1974), *Life Is Elsewhere* (1974), *The Farewell Party* (1976), *The Book of Laughter and Forgetting* (1980), and *The Unbearable Lightness of Being* (1984). Kundera uses his own experience to depict a divided world where the impulses of the soul are crushed by lies and where laughter offers the only way out. (Translator's note)

2. Manès Sperber (b. 1904) has published a three-volume autobiography, *Ces temps-là* (Paris: Calmann-Lévy, 1976–79), describing the tribulations of a Jew born in Eastern Galicia at the beginning of the century and tossed between Poland, the Ukraine, Austria, and Germany. He is a witness to the crisis which put an end to *Mittel Europa* and to its cosmopolitan culture. (Translator's note)

tance out of which the nations to which we belong were formed, an inheritance which is Byzantine, Latin, Greek, Germanic, and Hebrew. Christianity was the matrix for all these cultures and all these peoples. It is important to remember that and to make an inventory of our past because the secularist crisis of today is making us so shortsighted. Europe is being denied its true self by becoming blind to the world of thought. We must become aware of the real situation and learn about a dimension of our history which we ignore at our peril.

It is Europe which produced the apparatus of thought, of action, and of social living which have now been adopted by the whole world. Christianity had a part in their production. Sometimes this apparatus has turned against Christianity or has proved to be bad, but it is a product of Christianity nonetheless.

What is this apparatus?

First, there is *science produced by rational inquiry*. Europe is not the only civilization which produced science. It was present in China, in the Asiatic civilizations, and in the Arab world. But it is the rational thought and the technology of the West which are now dominant throughout the world with their norms, their criteria, and their products. This intellectual and technical way of doing things is imposing on the whole world a way of being which comes from the West; it is closely related to the origins of the West, of which Christianity was the matrix, that is, the formative mold.

Second, it was Europeans who *explored* our planet and *drew up the inventory of the human race*. The Japanese did not discover Europe; it was the Europeans who discovered Japan. The American Indians did not discover Europe; it was the Europeans who discovered America. Such undertakings and such successes are produced by the way people think of themselves and how they relate to others and to the world. Why are some societies unchanging? Why are other societies changing and bringers of change? It all has to do with the content of the mental structures of these societies which give them their framework.

But isn't it precisely this spirit of conquest which Europe is now being blamed for?

It is true that these great discoveries took the form of expanding colonialism. But don't forget the third element in the history of European nations, which is *the rule of law* at the service of the common good of human beings and their dignity as persons. This has become a universal ideal. But at the same time such an ideal has been used here and there to justify injustice and the denial of civil rights; what was a truth about humankind can be turned into one of its lies.

Thus science and technology, the discovery of the world and of the whole human race, democracy, all these are fundamentally linked to the way Europe inherited the Bible and the faith; Christianity was intended for all peoples and has been preached in fact to all the continents.

Fourth, behind the upheavals of the world, there lies a view of what society might be; it derives in part from an imperial ideology which is opposed to the idea of the kingdom of God and of the king-priest; it is presented to the peoples of the world as a blueprint which can be a means of improvement and development. Thus *the notion of development* is itself derived from Christian Europe, for better or worse.

You talked about a perversion of the Christian heritage in Europe. What do you mean?

If you look at the temptation of Christ in the desert and the story of the Exodus, you will see that they are archetypal; there you will see what I mean by a perversion. I mean by it the evil which only occurs when the good is shown up by the light of revelation and which tries to take its place by pretending to be good.

I have indicated what the benefits have been historically of the adherence by the nations of Europe to the grace of the covenant and of election in Jesus Christ. They have been scientific reasoning, the unity of our planet, and the kind of society which has emerged in Europe "from the Atlantic to the Urals" (I am quoting John Paul II, not General de Gaulle!). But all this power has been entrusted by God's creation and by his grace to human reason and freedom; it is to be used for the good of humankind but is in the keeping of people who are weak and sinful. Thus even the best gifts can lead to the worst perversions and confusions. But God, who is rich in mercy, can free the intelligence and the will of humankind once more from its sin and from its weakness. What we need for conversion is to acknowledge where our gifts come from and to confess our failures by name.

In view of what you have said about their inheritance and their failures, how do you think Europeans ought to behave?

The problems which were once confined to Europe have now been magnified to the scale of the whole planet and of humanity. This is further complicated by the fact that other living cultural traditions have either reacted against the influence of European culture or else have assimilated it. One can quite well imagine that our culture will one day be taken up by other human groupings who will change it deeply or reinterpret it.

But at the moment our responsibility to the rest of the world requires a fuller understanding of our own history, a sort of *anamnesis*. We need this in order to understand whether what we are doing is good or bad, whether it will benefit humanity or not. Where does our wealth come from? What causes our evil practices? If we answered these questions, we could to some extent put right our mistakes and exercise our responsibility.

To my mind, the diseases from which Europe suffers have something specifically Christian about them, at least in their origins. All nations have their idols. I would see the idols of the European nations as Christian ideas gone mad; they are reason taken to excess, the manipulation of communications, and the use of the power of the state against the community.

So would you say that the crisis of modern society is basically a Christian one?

At the center of this idol worship you will find a failure of faith. But only faith can cure the diseases of faith. Only a rediscovery of the Christian meaning of being human can enable Europe to cope with a modern way of thinking which is the product of Christianity.

Secularism is not a denial of God. It is the way an incarnate God challenges the clouded conscience of a believer. Thus technology and science only claim semidivine powers because human reason, from its understanding of God as creator, has transferred to them a sovereignty over the world which it would not otherwise have presumed to imagine. In the same way, the aims of those political regimes which are based on the principles of dialectic materialism can only be understood if one sees them as secularized eschatology; one can then understand that they are a contradiction and deny the very societies where they flourish. Racial and ethnic problems too arise only when the scattered elements of the human race are brought together, but it is the teaching of Christianity which calls them to acknowledge that they are all created as children of Adam. Thus all those deviations arise from temptations which come from the good things that humanity has received.

The duty of Europeans is to go back to the Christian roots of their culture so as to find a cure for all our current problems. We need that for the welfare of Europe but also because of our responsibility to the rest of the world.

Aren't you putting the blame on the whole of Europe's Christian past?

It is faith in God, who has given us his grace and has associated us in Jesus Christ with his promise of salvation, which will make it possible for us Europeans to become aware of our dignity as persons, created in the likeness of God and called to live as brothers and sisters by the freedom of his Spirit. It is by faith that we will be able to recognize the gifts of God which have come from the faith which our forebears had in the Gospel of salvation. It is by faith that we shall be able to discover in our cultural heritage that increase which was promised to our forebears who sought for justice.

But it is also faith which makes it possible for us to confess the faults committed against the gifts we have received; that is, our sins and their all-too-real results. By faith we can recognize the social and historical dimensions of the injustice and the violence which were committed in the name of the fatherhood of God and the brotherhood of man; they were committed in the name of such ideals as truth and the freedom of the Spirit. It is faith which makes it possible for us to give a name to the murderous lie which divides Europe, enslaves it and deludes it, under the mask of a dialectic materialist ideology. When we confess our faults, we are bringing to mind the Christian faith which made it possible for the continent of Europe to find unity in the diversity of its peoples. John Paul II proclaimed this in Vienna, at the very heart of Europe.

How do you see the churches taking part in the rediscovery of a specifically European identity and responsibility?

Let's come back to Central Europe. In France we have forgotten about it; we have been silent about the Communist domination which threatens the people of Central Europe.

But we cannot stifle the truth forever; people must speak out. One can see this today, even in Russia. The ancient culture which is a part of present-day Russia cannot be stifled. It is important not to connive in a conspiracy of silence; the violence which is destroying the identity of Europe must be called by its proper name.

And yet the nations have not entirely accepted this consigning to oblivion; the peoples of the East have not agreed to the denial of their social and European reality. I was very struck by this in Vienna and in Cracow, where it is very obvious. The churches can be for the peoples of Central Europe a guarantee that they are not forgotten and a pledge of their continued existence. These churches maintain their role as witnesses and means for the handing on of the ancestral faith; they are a sign of life for countries whose Christian past engendered their national identity.

There's another thing. Is there anyone who can gather crowds together like the pope, whether it be in Poland or in Latin America? He is the witness to a real *communio* which transcends the unforgivable divisions of the human race. They are unforgivable because they would deny the unity of humankind, the equality of its rights and duties, its vocation to the same divine destiny, whichever side of an ideological frontier it may come from. What the pope does is to defend, in the name of the redeemer of humankind, our basic and common humanity. In doing that, in witnessing to the humble condition of the believer, he is demonstrating the existence of a communion of believers which transcends the deep divisions of humanity.

It is the local churches, within the universal Church, which give reality to that communion, whatever the diversity of cultural life in each country and nation.

But in Europe there are not only Catholic bishops. . . .

I am talking both of Catholic bishops and of the bishops and leaders of the other Christian communities. The churches, by building up a sacramental community, are bringing reconciliation to the divided body of Europe. From that point of view, ecumenism in the proper sense is a task of major importance, especially ecumenism between the oriental Church and the churches of the West. The sacramental principle of communion and reconciliation also operates outside Europe. That same communion, which is being established by the cross within our divisions, holds together and unites the different parts of a human race which is threatened by war.

You mention war. Do you think that the community of Christians can be stronger than war?

The principle of our unity is the cross of Christ. The cross gives to believers, who are not necessarily political leaders, the means of an inner regeneration, just as a living tissue heals a wound. But this sharing in a new destiny does not operate only or even primarily at the level of political entities. It is not only nations that have to react against the deadly threat constituted by lying ideologies. It is the tissue of our personal commitments and of our social relations which is capable of regeneration. If the poor and the humble of our countries are able by faith to rediscover the basic values of forgiveness, love, and hope, and if they can practice them, then there will be a real change for the better in our history; the common good of our countries will thus be strengthened.

Historically our faith in the creator and redeemer, who conquered the world on the cross, remains the source of survival and renewal for our society under threat.

America: A Dream for Europe

Y ou Americans represented for Europe the hope of a new world. Both for those who crossed the Atlantic to go to these new territories and for those who stayed in the old country and dreamed about them, the new lands were not then thought of merely in terms of expansion for the old nations of Europe. On the contrary, they were the realization of a dream; your ancestors, having left nations grown old in their injustice, had the intention of bringing to birth a new people whose future would restore to humanity its primitive innocence. Their hope was that here below, beyond the oceans, a new heaven and a new earth could be reached. In those days they took with them to the Far West the hope of more than a thousand years, a hope which had been at the heart of the peoples of Europe since they had received with the grace of their baptism the treasure of the Word of God. That hope was such that your ancestors were convinced that it would come true at last in this new land and through their efforts. In the eighteenth century, the age of Enlightenment, America seemed to guarantee that a wild dream would come true and that human reason could bring to birth a new humanity. Thus it was that a rebellion, nourished on such dreams, became a revolution.

In the years following until today, this dream has inspired the revolutions which have shaken the peoples and nations of the world and continue to do so. The dream is the same, to bring forth a new humanity. The dream and the ambition have been the same from Western Europe to Eastern Europe and to the farthest parts of the continent of Asia.

How is it that this dream seems fated to produce its opposite? Why, both in the past and today, has it produced bloodshed and why has it failed? This question reechoes throughout the world. It is prompted by the innocent

An address given at the Cathedral of Notre-Dame de Paris on the occasion of the two-hundredth anniversary of the treaties of Versailles and of Paris, 2 September 1983.

blood shed on earth which cries out to God as did the blood of Abel. Only yesterday men and women were slain in the sky by other human beings?[1] and today everyone is looking for some justification for this madness.

How is it that the attempt to create a new humanity results all too often in the destruction of human beings? How is it that the search for freedom can produce their enslavement? How is it that the realization of their rights can be achieved at the cost of denying those very rights? I must ask myself those questions in this time and place, just as I ask them of you. It was after all the same movement for freedom and the same hope, which had produced the American nation, which led here in Paris to the decisive events of the French Revolution, shaking the Old World to its foundations as it awaited its renewal. The date was 14 July 1789.

There is another significant date: 2 September 1792. Not far from here is the house of the Carmelite fathers which has now become the seminary of the Catholic University of Paris, where I and many other priests were ordained.[2] On 2 September 1792 nearly two hundred Christians were put to death for their faith in that place; among them were nearly one hundred priests of the diocese of Paris. The Catholic Church has declared them to be martyrs and venerates them. Today is their anniversary and their feast day. I was struck by the coincidence that you have come to the cathedral of Paris on their anniversary. This underlines the urgency of my question: Why can humanity not be its own savior?

You Americans cannot ignore such a question either. Your own children, the offspring of Europe's dream, are scrutinizing their history. They are asking at what price these new territories were conquered and what happened to the ancient peoples who had lived there. What is more, you have had to pay very dearly for the rights and equality of those men and women who came to America, not to receive the gift of freedom at last, but who were brought from Africa as slaves. In the last fifty years you have had to relearn

1. During the night of 31 August–1 September 1983, a Korean Airlines plane on a flight from New York to Seoul which had gone off course entered Soviet airspace and was shot down with the loss of 269 lives. (Translator's note)

2. The house of the Discalced Carmelite friars in Paris was founded at the beginning of the seventeenth century, the first stone of the church being laid by Marie de Medici, Queen of France, in 1613. The church and the conventual buildings are at 70 Rue de Vaugirard on the south bank. At the time of the French Revolution they were used as a prison; on 2 September 1792 over one hundred bishops, priests, clerics, and one layman were summarily executed by the mob because they had refused to swear allegiance to the Civil Constitution of the Clergy, imposed on the French Church without the agreement of the Holy See. They were beatified by Pius XI in 1926. The buildings were taken over by the Catholic University of Paris on its foundation in 1875; the seminary attached to the university, known as the *Séminaire des Carmes*, occupies the conventual buildings. (Translator's note)

what you had perhaps forgotten (something that our age-worn wisdom in Europe has now allowed our nations to forget), that it is a duty to defend rights even at the cost of using force. But how difficult it is then to prevent right from being used in the service of force!

Well, we have to find an answer to that urgent question if experience does show that humanity is powerless to bring into being a new humanity. Does this mean that we have to give up the ideals which were indicated long ago by the birth of the United States of America? Must we accept the pitiless, despair-inducing hardness of our history, heartless and merciless though it be?

Your own history has given a partial answer to that question. When Benjamin Franklin came to plead your cause in Paris at the end of 1776 he brought tears to the eyes of the elite of our nation. He brought with him the Declaration of Independence of the United States of America of 4 July 1776; it was the first declaration of the rights of man. I would like to quote a phrase from this magnificent text: "all men are created equal . . . endowed by their Creator with certain inalienable rights." Here is the foundation which allows human beings to face their contradictions and their shortcomings. This is because the hope of which America became the bearer lies in this, that every human being is recognized as having the same fundamental rights. It is therefore of decisive importance for the future of humankind that the proclamation of these basic rights should be safeguarded from arbitrary tyranny. Such rights should not be subject to the fluctuations of majority opinion, at any time or place. It is therefore necessary to make it quite clear that they are not only the result of a pact freely entered into. They are not just the result of a social contract, even one which is deemed to have founded society. They come from a pact and a covenant which is even more basic than any freely undertaken human convention. Humankind does not have the power to modify this pact, because it is the covenant which binds to their creator human beings who have been created in the image and likeness of God. As your Declaration of Independence states, these rights are inalienable because it is God who has endowed human beings with them; thus has he endowed *all* human beings and it is not permissible for them to reduce or to limit such creative generosity, nor may they lose or alter it.

So here we have a vital question which is being asked everywhere today. Everybody knows that they have rights and everyone hopes that they will remain inalienable. But who will guarantee these rights? Where is the truth that will proclaim them? Where is the love that will reconcile them? It has taken us two hundred years to have a glimpse of what the hope of a new humanity and the proclamation of the rights of humanity could mean. Humanity, now that it has reached the end of the second millennium, has a confused feeling that it needs to receive in its heart the source of life so that it can achieve more than mere survival. It needs to receive the source of law so that it can act with justice. It needs to receive the source of truth in order to "proclaim Liberty throughout the Land to all the Inhabitants thereof," according to the phrase inscribed on the Liberty Bell at Philadelphia, which takes up an expression from the Book of Leviticus.[3]

To answer that question another lesson must be drawn out of the wealth of our history. We receive this lesson from the memory of the martyrs I mentioned at the beginning. Today's mass applies to them the readings from Scripture that we have just heard.[4]

These martyrs were not soldiers but victims. They were given the choice of saving their life if they were willing to give up that which gave them the reason for living. They preferred to die rather than lose their very selves by giving up their fidelity to God and the communion of the Catholic Church. So they left this world in order to remain true to the faith which gives them life even in death. They died giving a blessing, not a curse. In their weakness they forgave.

Contemporaries treated them as enemies; in fact they were friends. In the peaceful offering of their love was revealed the strength which God gives to men and women which makes it possible for them to defend human rights.

At this point in our meditation I would like to echo the words of John Paul II at Lourdes this year when he spoke to us during the night of 14 August. He was speaking to Christians all over the world and to all men and women; he wanted them to acknowledge that when the basic right to religious freedom is violated a signal has been given which makes it possible to see what attitude is being taken to all the rights of all human beings. He appealed to Christians, asking them to understand that the martyrdom which identifies them with Christ, their master, is also a witness to human rights and a defense of these rights. They are making a contribution by respecting these rights in their neighbor, even at the cost of their own life.

Thus does history reconcile those who have torn each other apart in the name of their rights. It reconciles them in the communion of love. Hope lives on, all the stronger for being founded on this covenant with the creator. It was the covenant which the American nation wished to inscribe on the tablets of its memory. It is the covenant which gives strength to the martyrs. It makes them peaceful upholders of all rights and witnesses finally to a love which can overcome death.

---

3. Lev. 25:10: "You shall hallow the fiftieth year and proclaim liberty throughout the land for all its inhabitants." (Translator's note)

4. The readings for the Feast of the Blessed Martyrs of the Carmes in the calendar of the diocese of Paris are 1 Pet. 3:14–17; John 15:18–21. (Translator's note)

Europe, the Pope, and Universality

*P*ope John Paul II emphasized at Compostella and at Vienna: "the unity of Europe will come through the faith."

That statement is perfectly obvious. At present Europe as it was in history has been broken in two by the opposition between East and West. For strategic and ideological reasons Germany has been divided to form two countries; this was done to curb the nation which twice this century dominated the continent. This calculated decision has had a result which is the opposite of what was intended by the conquerors of 1945. We are seeing the awakening of the German nation in spite of its being cut in two by the division of ideologies in Europe.

European nations have a common history which comes from the joining together of very different ethnic groups: Mediterranean peoples and those from Western Europe through to the Germanic and Slavic tribes which became Christian round about the tenth century. The basic mold which shaped these nations was created by the meeting of the Judaeo-Christian tradition with Greek and Latin civilization. So the unity of Europe is not the result of a political framework which looks to the future; it comes from a common lifestyle, a style of family life and conviviality almost, which stretches back into the past. The present state of division does violence to Europe and entails an enormous cultural loss for the whole of humanity. Europe is suffering as the result of its own faults; the ideological differences do not result from exterior force but are the product of European culture, that is, political utopias, the scientific spirit and the technological revolution which resulted from it and has now spread to the whole world. The United States and South America are essentially an outgrowth of Europe which transplanted its own form of slavery to the New World. Thus millions of

Answers to questions asked by the Brazilian newspaper *Veja*, 23 October 1983, reproduced in the *National Catholic Register*, Los Angeles, 16 September 1984.

African slaves were shipped to North and South America. The New World is paying today for that crime of the past. If the spirit of Christian fellowship is producing a greater good from the situation, that is according to the teaching of the faith. God can bring good from evil and he can do it for cultures and for history.

So you are carrying our hopes and our sins but you have in addition an illusion. The evils from which we suffer today are all the products of Europe: the grasping for wealth, materialism, the abuse of technology, totalitarian ideologies, especially Marxist ones, social utopias. Are these all enemies of Christianity and foreign to it? Not at all. These are the temptations of Christianity. These are the mistakes, the trials, the results, and the products of Christian nations.

To cure these evils it is necessary to return to the common origin. If a person of God and a believer sins, he or she can only assume the consequences by a deep conversion. As in the search for a cure, humanity must retrace its steps. It must come to see where it went astray, where it took a wrong turn, misunderstood what is possible and ignored part of the truth. Take the example of Marxism. It is an ideology which reversed Hegel's philosophy and fulfilled it. In fact Hegelianism itself was the satisfaction of a rational quest of which Christianity was the cause. Hegelianism was Christian theology secularized and turned upside down. We should therefore not be surprised at finding in Marxism as it exists a concentration of all the temptations of the human spirit in search of the absolute. If one wants to go back to the origin, all this must be converted. Certain Russian Christian thinkers of the twenties and thirties saw this very clearly; it is really a spiritual challenge.

Historically the fate of the whole of humankind is also being decided in Europe, though not only here. We Europeans are now facing problems which originally came from us and of which we have now become the victims. Thirty or forty years ago, before the terrible upheavals caused by Hitler and Stalin, we were still speaking in France of Central Europe as a cultural concept, not just a geographical one. Central Europe did mean of course the area from Germany to the Balkans, but it meant primarily the cultural unity which linked Paris, London, Milan, Rome, and Madrid to Weimar, Berlin, Cracow, Prague, Budapest, Sofia, and Moscow. That part of Europe was a laboratory of ideas; it was a theater for the arts and an oratory for the faith. It was unique and irreplaceable. Its disappearance has wounded Western Europe so that we have become like a branch cut off from its trunk. We are not really a European culture anymore, even though French culture was for a time a leaven for Europe, from Moscow to Berlin. Short indeed has been our memory in forgetting that part of Europe, whereas the people of the East are conscious of it and remember. Sometimes the people of the New

World know it better than we do; sometimes they have forgotten it completely.

*The Pope comes from the other side of Europe. Do you see him as bringing the
possibility of unity?*

I hope so. The very fact that he is there has made the walls of separation
crack. The common basis of European culture, which is Christianity, has
begun to appear more clearly and people are more conscious of it.

Has something changed already from the practical point of view?

Could I sum up very briefly? The cardinals made their decision in electing a
new pope. It was made in their secret conclave and reflects the secret plans of
God, on which one can only speculate. Through that decision, a whole area
of the Church which had been buried, if not forgotten, suddenly reappeared
in the light of day as far as Westerners were concerned.

Something struck me very much at the time of the election of John Paul II.
I had met in Paris some Vietnamese boat people. They were weeping with
joy when they heard who had been elected. I asked them why. They said:
"Because he knows what it is to have lost one's homeland. He is a Pole. He
will understand us. You French people cannot understand us." I was surprised by that and upset; it was clear that Polish Catholicism, because of what
it had been through, had become the symbol of survival for all those parts of
the Church which are hidden and misunderstood. In the same way the speech
of John Paul II at Lourdes on 14 August 1983 is of great importance because
it reminds the churches of the West that persecution is the normal situation
for the Church when it fulfills its mission.

Another thing which is characteristic of this pope is that through him
modern culture is being deliberately introduced into Christian thought. As
examples of this I would mention that in the summer of this year there was a
meeting at Castel Gandolfo, the papal summer residence, of university teachers from Germany, France, and Poland. Among them were Catholics, Protestants, Jews, and atheists; they discussed scientific and philosophical topics on
which the pope wanted to be informed. I would also mention the Wednesday
talks in which the pope meditates on our condition as created beings; if you
look at the footnotes you will see that the pope quotes most of the great
thinkers of today. There is a wide university culture which underlies his
thought. We have a pope who has read the great writers of today in the
original languages. This modern approach is not just something bookish. It
comes from the experience of a Church which has had to face the onslaught
of the ideologies of today; it has faced up to Marxism and its fantastic and
superhuman attempt to establish human mastery over social life. No other
Western country could produce a pope with experience of a Church which
has been crushed by the war, persecuted by the Nazis, which has had to fight
to maintain its national identity and which faces real socialism in a daily

confrontation since 1944. John Paul II today is the "most modern of Europeans" (and of others too) in the phrase which Guillaume Apollinaire[1] applied to Pius X.

Third, this pope has as his aim to apply Vatican II; he has said this clearly ever since his first speech. He does it boldly and strongly. His decision to go and visit churches in various countries is clearly a way for them to reach their full Catholic dimension. When John Paul II visits a country, the important thing is not what he sees but that the churches gather to welcome the pope; thus these churches become fully conscious of themselves. The coming of the pope makes men and women take stock and think; it challenges the churches to think out what they are and how they stand in relation to the world; in other words, to exist more fully. What he says in each country about current problems he says in conjunction with the local episcopate; he respects it, consults it, and never contradicts it. The pope comes as bishop of Rome and successor of Saint Peter, "the vicar of Peter" as he said again only recently. In that role he has the right to speak to a whole nation and to its bishops to whom he brings comfort, help, respect, and encouragement.

Finally, it is important to emphasize that the pope gets across to people that Christianity has something to say about humanity as such. This is important for the Church and for human conscience generally. John Paul II teaches a doctrine on humanity as such and at the same time powerfully explains its predicament in the light of Christian revelation. He does not expound a general sort of philosophy which would be acceptable independently of the faith. When he talks about human beings, he starts from Christ as redeemer, Christ as the perfect image of God, and Christ as the only way by which created humanity can discover itself. Thus his anthropology derives from his Christology and can only be taken in and accepted by the act of faith. This is why his first encyclical was called *Redemptor Hominis;* one of the latest ones is on God's mercy as bringing forgiveness and the power of love instead of the violence of conflict (conflict is the Hegelian approach as applied to states and social relations). The pope's anthropology implies a basic self-surrender, but this is becoming acceptable now, even outside the Catholic Church, because we are at a time when men and women are experiencing a crisis about the nature of humanity.

So Pope John Paul II comes as a witness; as a witness he is a believer and he is to be believed. He is a witness to something universal, to the complete Human Being, to Christ. Thus does he define the role that each Christian has to play in the world of today.

1. Guillaume Apollinaire (1880–1918) was a surrealist poet. His collected poems, *Alcools: Poèmes 1898–1913* (Paris: Gallimard), contain the verse:

> *Seul en Europe tu n'es pas antique ô Christianisme*
> *l'Européen le plus moderne c'est vous Pape Pie X*

(Translator's note)

THE THIRD WORLD AND ITS SPIRITUAL WEALTH

—✳—

What Price Development?

In the rich countries of the world we seem to be brimming over with the sumptuous beauty of life. We are bursting with all the riches of the world and with everything needed to bring joy to life. The earth seems to be in our hands. But it does not belong to us. The whole earth comes from God who has entrusted it to all of us.

We, the rich countries, have drawn to ourselves for our profit the life of the whole world. That is why we are perhaps already dead, because we are in the process of losing our soul.

At this very moment the majority of people on our earth are condemned to die of famine, poverty, or disease. Their fragile cultures are collapsing because we dominate them and put them under such pressure to provide for our progress.

But if this is the case, our civilization is condemning itself to death. We are abandoning our dignity as human beings if we are prepared to deny to less developed countries their dignity as children of God and to control for our own profit the whole world and its wealth instead of recognizing that God has given it to all for their happiness. If we take away the dignity of human beings from our brothers and sisters, we lose our own.

Our own soul dies through the death of our brethren. Thus the more advanced countries are dying through the death of the less developed ones. A rich country which has lost its soul is a nation of dead people. A luxurious culture without a soul is a dead culture.

Any economic system which leaves millions of people dying in appalling conditions is a system of death, whatever intentions it may have for promoting greater justice.

As for a country whose soul has died, a culture without reasons for living,

A talk given at the prayer meeting in the Church of St. Francis Xavier in Paris on the occasion of the Conference for Less Developed Countries, 9 September 1981.

economic and social systems which go against the very aims they are supposed to serve, all these can only produce nothingness and destruction. In fact this is what we can see around us. What price the progress of the more developed countries?

There are countries threatened by death because children are not born anymore; there are developed countries where youth give way to despair, where self-indulgence is constantly being provoked by advertisements in the interests of consumption and production. In other developed countries human freedom and culture are curtailed because they are subjected to powerful egalitarian ideologies. In some developed countries all the resources of science and wealth are employed for the production of death-dealing weapons. Who are we so afraid of, that we stockpile all our resources in weapons of death instead of spending them in generous giving and the sharing of all this wealth?

Those among you who are Christians will have recognized the words of Jesus Christ himself: "What will it profit a man if he gain the whole world and forfeits his life? Or what shall a man give in return for his life?" (Matt. 16:26)

Time is running short. But perhaps it is not too late and our historical culture can still be saved from the deadly disease which is eating our heart away. It is indeed a deadly disease and it kills twice over since it is destroying our brothers and sisters and leading us to suicide.

If we want to survive, each and every one in our society must be prepared to show greater generosity; only thus will our dignity be restored, because it is only if we are prepared to share with these men and women, our brothers and sisters, that we shall really become their brothers and sisters. We shall then receive what constitutes the fundamental dignity of human beings and their vocation.

My words here have been addressed to the more developed nations because the threat of a spiritual death is closer to them and their plight is more urgent; whereas the threat of physical death is more immediate for less developed countries. Your conference is trying to find ways of controlling economic, social, and cultural factors so as to help the less developed countries; this is a difficult thing to do and it will make a greater respect for human beings possible. But in doing this you are also facing up to the most serious threat which hangs over the more developed countries, which is the collapse of their spiritual values. Like the colossus with the feet of clay (Dan. 2:31–35), they are threatened with destruction but now it is a case of self-destruction.

To you, my brothers and sisters from the underdeveloped countries where people are dying of hunger and thirst, where life is short and uncertain, where disease is rampant, I say that you must preserve your dignity as human beings because it has been given to you by God. Therein lies your wealth and your strength. You are the only ones who can give our dignity back to us.

The Face of the Future

John Paul II is setting out on his pilgrim road again and this time to Africa. Is this just a coincidence? It could be, but I think that it is significant that the pope, having escaped death from the attempt on his life, will be once more witness to the unity of the Church at a time when his homeland is going through an unbearable ordeal yet again. But for us Europeans as for the people of Africa, he is an example of the unbelievable change in attitudes which has occurred in less than a hundred years.

Thus people in the nineteenth century thought of the African continent as a place of death and they considered black people under a curse. Today what we are worried about is its growth rate. This continent which has had such a late start seems to be condemned for a long time to hunger, disease, and internal instability; although those who know it well would state things with more reservation and can point to positive aspects for the future of Africa.

This crisis of human dying can be seen as the counterpart of our spiritual death. We, the rich countries, have drawn all this material wealth to ourselves. Perhaps that is why we are already dead; we are losing our soul. Our civilization is signing its own death warrant by not allowing Africans to have an equal dignity as children of God and by trying to grab the material resources of the whole earth. When we try to take away from our brothers and sisters their dignity as human beings, then we lose our own. Our soul dies by their death. The more developed countries die by the death of the less developed countries.

In our society each and every one must accept a greater generosity if we are to recover our own dignity. I have said this to the Conference of the United Nations for Developing Countries. I will go on saying it. If we accept to

An article in *Le Monde,* 12 February 1982.

share with those who are our brothers and sisters, then we ourselves receive that which constitutes a human being's fundamental dignity and vocation.

When I recently visited an African church for the first time, in Senegal, a great hope came upon me. On African soil the young black churches are giving us outstanding examples of overflowing vitality. These peoples, when they accept the Gospel, produce results which astonish the very ones who have brought them the seeds of truth; and this in spite of being weak and "backward" countries struggling with poverty. Even in its present precarious situation, Christian Africa constitutes the hope of a renewed youthfulness and the face of the future for our old Christian countries which seem so tired and worn out. Africa is already giving back a hundredfold what it has received, and this is according to the law of God's gifts.

If one is prepared to acknowledge this spiritual fruitfulness and to welcome it in hope, then one will acknowledge the fundamental unity of the human family and its solidarity. The black person, who seems so strange and so different from us, is the younger child in the faith who receives as much love as the elder child; in fact he or she makes it possible for the firstborn to rediscover the gift which he or she received first and then got used to. Thus is the stranger accepted, not only as someone like ourselves, but as the gift of God who is giving back to us the understanding of our own basic dignity. So among the churches we are living as equals, even though we are in a world where there is inequality in the field of economics and politics, an inequality which is unfortunately reinforced by armed strength. The poorer churches bestow on the richer ones from their very poverty the superabundance of what they have just received. The last have become first. The workers who were taken on at the end of the day receive the same pay as those who were taken on at the first hour.

This is something that we are experiencing in the relations between the dioceses of France and those of Africa, but not enough is being done. On our side we still look at things with the attitude of the colonial period when they were dependent on us; we are wrong about this. It is surprising for a French person to discover in certain African churches today that the history of the missionaries is proudly assumed by the Christians of Africa as being their own history; we are apt to try and forget it as tainted by colonialism or racism.

The Africanization of Christianity creates a problem for Europeans. But many Africans are experiencing it with the instinctive wisdom which accepts in complete fidelity that growth will be slow. Perhaps there is a true realism here that we still have to learn from them. We have already received from these African churches, which are so generous and so full of initiatives, the fresh inspiration of which we are perhaps running short.

In Africa John Paul II will help us to see that the Church is young; that is something that French Catholics used to dream about. But there is a youthfulness which is perpetually being called forth by the Gospel. When the pope visited us, he asked: "France, what have you done with your baptism?" In order to hear this question aright and to give it an answer, perhaps we need the help of those young sister churches to whom we brought baptism not so long ago.

Servants of All Our Brothers and Sisters

W e have been warned that drought and famine are inevitably going to cause very many deaths in the months and years to come. Is this something inevitable that we can do nothing about? Can our rich countries just say that they are noncombatants when faced with a scourge which is certain to claim so many victims?

We cannot accept such a thing because all men are involved here, not because the survival of the whole human race is in question; it has survived many other bloodlettings. But what is in question is the respect which everyone owes to other persons. What is in question is the solidarity which links every individual to all the others because we have been created in the image and likeness of God and, as children of the same Father in heaven, we are brothers and sisters. So as Christians we are not entitled to consider the present threat as inevitable.

This is what brings you together today, your stubborn refusal to accept what is going on in Africa and your hope founded on an act of faith. I am aware of the different places you come from and the variety of the work you do for the Church in parishes, chaplaincies, movements, and so on. Your very presence reminds us that in our country, which is so rich, there is this refusal to accept fate as inevitable; it is an urgent and persistent reminder. Whereas those who are experts in the field of development, the specialists and the international civil servants, are admitting defeat and giving way to doubt,

A contribution to the Ile-de-France section of the CCFD (*Comité Catholique contre la Faim et pour le Développement,* the official organization set up by the Church in France for help to the Third World), published in *Paris Notre-Dame,* no. 18, 16 March 1984.

you persist in your faith and your hope that eyes can be opened and that the human heart can be changed by the Spirit of God.

Your campaign, carried on in humility, elicits the generosity of all the members of the Church, including those who are satisfied with the silent offering of small sums of money. You have learned that such people must not be despised, since the sums of money entrusted to you include the widow's mite, given by one who for the love of God offers everything she had to live on. You know this. You are therefore responsible, before the Church and before God, for more than a sum of money; what is in your keeping is the generosity inspired by God in your brothers and sisters in the faith in spite of all the despair in the world.

That is why I must give you further strong words of encouragement. You are facing up to the scandal of so much evil, the suffering of so many people now dead, the bitterness and the revolt caused by so much injustice. May this burden not crush you or harden you. The material means entrusted to your hands are as yet insufficient to solve the problem, but they are given to you by the Church, that is, by the multitude of your brothers and sisters, with the understanding that you must be, among them and in their name, those who persevere in bringing a message of love. Because it is only love which can open hearts that are closed and hands which clutch their paltry riches. In the name of the compassion of Christ, you must be the witnesses of a love which is stronger than all the will to possess and to have power.

What you have learned in fact is the humble and hidden way of love. Thus does love work to break up the granite of selfishness. The weapons of violence crush and destroy but in doing so they destroy themselves. The weapons of love are infinitely more powerful, precisely because they are weaker. They do not destroy; they build up because they are able to reach the root cause of all these calamities in the evil which lies in the human heart; this is the teaching of the Second Vatican Council in its pastoral constitution *Gaudium et Spes*.[1]

All this explains clearly the reasons which led the Church in France to set up a technical organization like your own which could serve the Church's own institutions, its associations and parishes. This organization can only be and should only be the servant and the working arm of the powerful urge to love which dwells at the heart of the Church. It must be a technical means for all Christians, whatever their background and their analysis of the situation, whatever their outlook or their convictions in this field. Thus will they be

---

1. "The Word of God . . . reveals to us that God is love and at the same time teaches that the fundamental law of human perfection, and consequently of the transformation of the world, is the new commandment of love" (*Gaudium et Spes*, no. 38, in *Vatican Council II: The Conciliar and Post Conciliar Documents*, edited A. Flannery [Dublin, 1975], p. 937). (Translator's note)

enabled as efficaciously as possible to take on the responsibility of becoming in Christ the servants of their brothers and sisters.

We can thus begin to see the answer to a question which is rightly asked of us by governments and nonreligious agencies: "Why is there a specifically Catholic organization in the fight against hunger and for development? Why can't everyone of goodwill get together on the basis of humanitarian concern alone?"

I am sure that you are convinced that it would be misleading for ourselves and for all our fellow Catholics to answer that the only aim of such an organization is to raise funds more easily. You know that it is part of our identity as Catholics to put ourselves at the service of all people, our brothers and sisters, in the way Christ became our servant for the salvation of all to the glory of God the Father.

You know that the love of the Father in heaven has been revealed in his Son and is made present in the world by Christ's brothers and sisters who have received the Holy Spirit. Thus do they, even when they belong to opposing groups and to nations which are hostile to each other, constitute a unique community here and now. The unity of Christians cuts across all boundaries and challenges all human conflicts. This Christian and ecclesial community is a powerful means toward achieving communion for a truly human fellowship. Already as Christians we experience in the Church complete fellowship and equality, in spite of differences, inequalities, and conflicts. This happens by the power of the Spirit of the Risen One and at the cost of accepting his cross.

This communion in Christ is of major importance for the future of a human race which is divided and torn apart. It is the prophetic sign of a hope which Christians must follow up by proving that it is a possibility. This message is greater than we are. It is the message of the love of Christ; the Father in heaven gives witness to it through his Son and through our lives, in spite of our weakness and our limitations. You must therefore be conscious of the fact that the search for a solution to the world problem of development leads by way of Christian communion and ecclesial solidarity.

For Catholic organizations this solidarity implies necessarily the respect and love of all our Christian brothers and sisters; it implies a real communion with the churches of the various countries and continents, not something which remains at the level of tactics only; it implies the same respect in equality for each and every one of these local churches. It is a condition of our fidelity to our own ideal that we carry this out conscientiously; to do otherwise would be to make our wealth, our gifts, our know-how instruments of power and domination hidden under a cloak of service. Thus do we find our special calling among the large number of organizations which are dealing with the same sort of problems; God requires of us that we give a sign of hope for the whole world; that sign is Christ.

So everyone here should be convinced that what he or she does for the fight against famine and for human development is much more important than what is immediately and visibly achieved. I wish you all plenty of courage; I pray for you in friendship.

YOUTH AND SCHOOL

These Young People Are the Church

ou said once that youth are encamped at the gates of society. Do you think that the Church is going to lose the young people to today as it has lost the working class?

The Church does not lose young people any more than do their parents or our national system of education.

Christians have within them the resources they need, if God wants and if they want to, for responding to the demands of young people. Not losing the youth does not mean taking them in. It doesn't mean organizing them on a massive scale. The youth of today belong to nobody; nor do old people for that matter. Human beings belong to God; and what God wants is that they should belong to themselves.

Since you were for a long time chaplain to students at Paris University, I suppose you know these young people well, the ones from an intellectual background.

Western Europe is made up of aging countries. Age is a problem. The evidence for that is the state that young people are in. When a country is no longer able to transmit what it lives by to its younger generation, then that country is in the process of dying.

Do you think this is the case?

One can ask the question. When a culture is no longer able to pass on its reasons for living, this proves that these reasons are no longer strong enough or lively enough to be accepted by the next generation. What begins then is a sort of death of society, a collective dying, the end of a whole system of values. Whether one likes it or not, this is what is happening, and it's not a recent phenomenon either. For a long time the survival of the West has been in question. Don't forget that the first thing that the totalitarian ideologies of the West did was to try to regiment young people. Youth was taken in by these illusions and it swore that it would not be taken in again.

An interview with Robert Serrou in *Paris-Match,* 4 April 1981.

Well, what has the Church to say to young people? What is it telling them?

What I find wonderful and surprising is that young people themselves are defending the identity of the Church. They want to belong to the Church and they are the Church. If you search for the greatest vitality in the Church you will find it among young people. They are grasping with both hands the riches which have been given up by others. This does not refer necessarily to all young people in France, but there are countless groupings of young people, all sorts of new foundations which seem rather strange sometimes, all sorts of community movements which cover a great variety of activities, some of them rather extreme.

But what does all this add up to? A drop in the ocean?

Have you ever heard of active minorities?

I don't see youth as having much influence in the Church.

Of course it has. It is the part that is really lively.

I would like to believe you, but the young people I know are totally indifferent to the Church.

There was a time, about ten years ago, when people still thought that Christian milieus could transmit their practice and their beliefs as a whole to their children. That seems over now.

And yet!

More or less anyway. But it is among young people nowadays that initiative is to be found; this is where the true face of the Church appears. I have seen them and listened to them. Young people from all sorts of different communes have come to see me. They are sharing their money, their prayer life; they are quite mad! If they listened to us they would not be doing such silly things, the sort of things that Saint Francis of Assisi did. There is something wonderful about their imprudence. They must not be disillusioned. We must make sure, if we can, that their mistakes do not break them. Even if this small group of people is not going to set up among their contemporaries a new area of social conformity, what they are doing is discovering a new way of being in the Church.

It has always been like that. Look at the great spiritual revivals of the past. Saint Francis of Assisi had ten people as his first followers; Saint Ignatius had seven or eight; it was the same with Saint Benedict and Saint Bernard.

Do you think there are still people like Saint Bernard around today?

They are around allright, though most people don't know it and sometimes they don't know it either. They have already taken up the challenge. The Church of the third millennium is already in existence.

We Get the Youth We Deserve

oung people today are finding it difficult to believe in Christianity. Don't you find a growing gap between today's culture and the teaching of the Church?

Yes and no. Yes, in the sense that there are fewer young people going to church proportionally than there were twenty or thirty years ago.

But the real problem is not that there is a gap between the Church and young people; the problem is that young people do not have their place in society. On this I would like to say three things.

First, we get the youth we deserve. Young people today are not really loved; excuse me for making what may appear to be a cruel comment. These young people have not been loved and willed for themselves. In the West we have entered a period of sterility in which young people are not welcomed as a gift from God; they are not seen as our posterity and as the future freely given to us.

When youth is welcomed as a gift from God, then the first duty is transmitting to them love, life, and the values one believes in.

But in the West today we have children when we can afford it, just as we buy a car. So a child becomes an object; one can want to own it and one can refuse to have it. Some people refuse to have children because they think that the world is so awful.

How does such a situation have an impact on the faith of young people?

They know that they are not loved, that they are not wanted for themselves and that they do not have their place. As a result, they have no desire to accept the values that we want to transmit. They feel rejected by those very values.

If we want young people to have the faith, they must first of all be loved.

Now comes my *second* point: today's generations are deeply wounded.

What do you mean exactly?

An interview with Yves de Gentil-Baichis, published in *La Croix,* 31 October 1981.

They are wounded in their affective life, in their psychological balance and in the structure of their personality. You find the same thing in the United States, in Germany, and, I think, in the Anglo-Saxon countries.

The clearest signs of all this are to be seen in drug addiction, juvenile delinquency, and the number of people on the margins of society. What we have is a younger generation which is paying for the shortcomings of others which they themselves do not deserve. They have been damaged in all sorts of ways for which they are not responsible; I mean the instability of the family, the changes in social living, all sorts of tensions, and so on.

So all this makes it difficult of course for them to discover the faith?

Yes. Just as education is becoming very difficult, so is any tranquil growth into the life of faith. It is true that the faith as a spiritual experience can occur in any psychological situation, but it is nevertheless helped by a good education, in the general sense of the term.

If one wants to transmit the faith to young people, one immediately comes up with the problem of *salvation;* I am using the term in the most general sense. There is a whole process of *salvation* to be carried out among young people from the point of view of their health and to heal the traumas that they have suffered in their affective life.

Finally, my *third* point. We live in a consumer society where the aim of production is consumption. If desire increases, so will production. The promotion of sexual desire has now become something commercial. As I see it, permissiveness in sexual matters is a result of having a consumer society. The link between business and erotic desires is that both of them are subject to promotion.

What effect does this have on individuals?

It produces a wild imbalance. I was talking about this recently to Lech Walesa and his judgment on the West was extremely harsh. He said: "You have everything. You grab material things and yet you are not happy. We have nothing and yet we are happy. Why is that?"

Don't let us forget that youth are a prime target for those who produce and who promote the consumer society. At the same time society as a whole cannot give them reasons for living, and the Church to which their parents belong seems to them to be just another part of this society.

But don't you think that there is also a gap between the Christian faith and modern attitudes because the latter are conditioned by a technical, rational, and scientific approach and thus geared to what is immediately practical?

Yes, that's right. There's a big gap here and it is perhaps one of the weaknesses of our society. People's minds are formed in a certain way; everything to do with symbolism, feelings, relations, and personal life is marginalized and treated as irrational.

Would you say as archbishop of Paris that it's possible to reverse this trend?

If there's a problem about the faith of young people, it's because there's already a problem about the faith of adults. Faith can only be transmitted to young people if their parents accept a complete Christian life which is prepared to face all problems. Christianity cannot be limited to being just a part of life. You cannot strengthen faith by increasing the hours that it is taught in school, as you can with German or math. Christianity concerns the whole of life and young people know that; if faith does not transform the whole of life, young people can soon see the contradiction between their spiritual ideals and the sort of life adults are living.

What should we be doing to re-create this complete Christian life?

What we need to do is discover a new lifestyle. We have to accept that we are swimming against the tide; we need to find a lifestyle which is life giving and life enhancing.

I don't mean that we should re-create an entirely Christian society, separate from our own society. That was the temptation of the hippies in the sixties and seventies; they tried to live apart from the world which they had rejected. In our pitiless society, it is a temptation to which all religious revival movements are prone. Christians are not asked to flee but to be more active in making their contribution so that society can be changed.

More effort is needed to love than to fight against one's enemy. So Christians need to show that they can love more. Their love must be strong enough to survive in a society which denies love. Their love must make them into living signs of love for those who do not know what love is.

So to be a Christian in any real sense is a very costly business. It takes a lot of time, not just an hour a week. Christians have to make choices which are different from other people's. They cannot just conform to society as it is today; they have to discover a rationale which comes from God. They need the courage to share with the poorest and to welcome those who are awkward and importunate. They must discover new ways of praying in which everyone can really take part.

So what we need today is extra energy and extra love in order to live the kind of holiness which has to be discovered in relation to the world around us. That is true for us and it's true for young people.

Would you say that one can already see some indication that this new Christian lifestyle is being discovered?

Yes, there are some indications throughout the world. I am thinking of what is happening in Poland; I have seen in African Christians who, in the midst of all their difficulties, are inventing a new lifestyle based on the generosity of love and faith.

Foreigners tell us French that our Christianity is without joy. But I hope that it is just a case of love being under the surface; a spark will set the fire blazing again. That spark could come from a young person called by God. Remember what happened to Saint Francis of Assisi!

Youth at the Gates of Society

When you became archbishop of Paris a year ago you said: "The young are encamped at the gates of society." I want to ask you three things. First, what exactly did you mean? Second, couldn't you just as well have said: "The young are encamped at the gates of the Church"? Third, what can be done to welcome them into a society they are dropping out of and into a Church they don't believe in?

Well, there's a clear question anyway. It concerns the place which the young ought to have in the organization of society. In saying that, I am not accusing society. When I say that youth is camping at the gates, I mean that society is breaking up and the Church is a part of that society. So there is an internal problem. Society is threatened with death because its fruitfulness is in question; fruitfulness is a condition of life, and not just a physical condition either. The very values of our society are threatened from within. If values are not handed on, they die. Such values already carry the seeds of death and they are no longer able to welcome the values of life. Life tends to propagate itself, so here we have one of the most serious problems of our society. It is a diagnosis which affects its future. Youth are affected in the same way as adults. I think that the problems of youth are the problems which adults have too, though in a different way.

All this shows that society, insofar as it is becoming sterile, cannot ensure its own future. It cannot hand on its values; it is spiritually sick. A sign of this is the absence of any knowledge of history among the young; another sign is the way they reject their parents' lifestyle. This is a very serious spiritual problem for our society. It is a problem for everybody, whether they are believers or atheists, and of course it is a problem for Christians first of all.

Some people blame the clergy for this. People say they have not come to terms with their peripheral role in a secular society.

An interview with Robert Van Beselaere, published in *L'Ami du XXe*, March 1982.

These are difficulties facing the Church and the whole of society. I don't think that pastors should bear the blame more than anybody else.

Exterior signs, which used to symbolize our roots, have disappeared. You can't see our churches anymore. One of the powerful symbols of our society used to be the church steeple; it was used as such on some of the posters of the last election campaign. But in France there are no churches on the new housing estates; a large percentage of our population has gone to live there but, for various reasons including the lack of vitality perhaps on the part of Catholics, no churches were built. The Church has physically disappeared. So nowadays over half those who are under twenty do not have the Church as part of their mental horizon. That is a terrible break in French culture and tradition. People only think of the Church as part of the village life of their parents or grandparents. Perhaps there is nostalgia for a past way of life but there has been a terrible discontinuity over the last twenty years.

The literature produced by the Church after the Second World War shows that there was at the time a firm Christian base and a stable tradition. You can see this if you read *France, pays de mission?* by Godin, *Paroisse, communauté missionaire* by Michonneau, and the pastoral letters of Cardinal Suhard.[1] They were all worried about dechristianization, but it was nothing compared to what has happened in the last twenty years for various sociological reasons.

Today catechists know just how large is the proportion of young people who know nothing about Christianity. It just does not exist for them. In these cases it is not young people who are camped at the doors of the Church but it is the grown-ups who have not made the Church part of the world of young people.

That's worse, isn't it, because the transmission of values is done by adults!

Historically there has been a break and I don't see any short-term measures of a scale sufficient to change the situation. You cannot avoid the consequences of such a state of affairs. Of course the transmission of a certain number of Christian values through our culture was not necessarily a deep experience of faith. There has always been a gap between a deeply committed

---

1. Henri Godin (1906–44) was a priest and chaplain to the Young Christian workers. Published in 1943, *France, pays de mission?* drew attention to the fact that France could no longer be considered a Christian country.

Georges Michonneau (1900–38) was a parish priest of Colombes in the suburbs of Paris. His book *Paroisse, communauté missionaire* emphasized the missionary priorities of a parish community.

Emmanuel Suhard (1874–1949), archbishop of Paris (1940–49), set out the tasks facing the French Church in a series of widely acclaimed pastoral letters: *Essor ou déclin de l'Église* (1947), *Le sens de Dieu* (1948), and *Le prêtre dans la cité* (1949). Cf. *The Church Today: The Collected Writings of E. C. Suhard* (Chicago, 1953). (Translator's note)

Christian conscience and the assumptions of a society which were compatible with all sorts of ideological positions.

However, it was still true as late as the beginning of this century that anticlerical teachers were operating in a Christian society. I was at a state primary school as a child and our teachers were certainly not Catholics. Nevertheless, the moral teaching which they gave me was basically Christian, whether one likes it or not.

So we are still in the West!

Yes, Western civilization is marked by its Christian origins.

On Immaturity

Now the cardinal-archbishop of Paris is coming to what he considers as the most serious problem, the collapse of morality and the fall in the birthrate. He is going to look at these not from the demographic point of view but from the moral aspect.

The question I ask myself is this: What does the child stand for in the consciousness of a nation when one has reached such a stage? What it must mean is that the population as a whole does not believe in its future. The future should not be simply thought of in terms of retirement (and incidentally people tend to forget the sad side of retirement, death and decay). If people think of themselves as immortal, never seriously face death, and refuse to hand on life to a new generation, it is clear that there is already something seriously wrong. Society becomes static and is quite happy looking at itself in the mirror. This is a deadly falling back on oneself. This is the cause of the crisis of young people. They belong to a nation which has no future and so they cannot identify with anyone. They cannot be themselves because they find no points of reference in their elders who are so lacking in generosity.

Don't you find on the contrary that the idea of the family is becoming stronger, whereas it was considered badly shaken twenty years ago?

I really don't know. I was struck by the Sullerot Report.[1] The way young people behave today means that institutions are very weak because everything

---

An interview with Patrick Poivre d'Arvor in *Le Journal du Dimanche,* 4 March 1984.

1. Evelyne Sullerot (b. 1924), editor of a collective work, *Le fait féminin* (1978). In 1984 she edited a report, *Le statut matrimonial, ses conséquences juridiques, fiscales et sociales,* commissioned by a government body, the *Counseil Economique et Social.* The Sullerot Report was highly critical of French legislation as unfavorable to family life, child development, and the future of the population of the country. (Translator's note)

depends on the emotional state of the couple. They won't accept anything from institutional or social considerations.

Does that matter?

Human beings will pay for it in the long run. It will cause emotional traumas and breakups. From the psychological point of view, there is something recessional in the way the life of a couple is identified with a lyrical emotional state where two people find total communion and are almost fused into one. Such expectations cause immaturity; they show up a whole generation. Just look at the difference between the trials of adolescents and those of adults. The sufferings of adolescents provide great literary models (young Werther, *le Grand Meaulnes,* Coppola's latest film *Rusty James*),[2] but adolescence is a passing stage of human life which leads on to adulthood and one must know how to leave it behind. You cannot have a whole society which remains at the adolescent stage and produces only teenagers; if it does, it will perish. It is bad when people try to eliminate death. The only form of death which one sees nowadays is death on the television screen; it serves to provide drama or to reinforce guilt. Have a look at the study of the subject by Philippe Ariès;[3] he has just died, incidentally.

Should one complain about such a state of affairs?

I think one should. Nobody today ever sees a corpse. That is a dangerous state of affairs for the living. It means that one can fantasize about life with impunity. A son will only see his father or mother dead in hospital, and even this is not certain. Thus the reality of facing death, which is basic to human life, is ignored. The different generations are pulled apart. But a young person needs to know about old age, to respect the old. One should not hide away the sick, the wounded, and the handicapped. Those who face death tomorrow or the day after will be you and me. One has to face up to it; it is not as terrible as all that.

Do you see drugs as part of the crisis of society that you wish to condemn?

I do. There is a pressure group which would like to change the law and make drugs legal. That's bad. I am opposed to legalizing drugs in the way the Spaniards have done. It is for Christians to back up a critical judgment on the

---

2. "Young Werther," hero of Goethe's novel *The Sorrows of Young Werther* (1774), commits suicide through the despair of unrequited love.

Le Grand Meaulnes (1913) was the only novel of Alain-Fournier who was killed the following year on the western front during World War I; its subject is the emotional experiences of an adolescent.

Rusty James (1983) by the American film director Francis Ford Coppola is the story of the tragic adventures of adolescents fascinated by motorbikes. (Translator's note)

3. Philippe Ariès (1914–84), French historian, author of *The Hour of Our Death* and *Centuries of Childhood: A Social History of the Family.* (Translator's note)

question. The thing that strikes me above all in our society is conformity and the loss of independent judgment.

As one of the leaders of Christians in France, what is your comment on the amazing changes brought about by biology? There are now so many ways of having children apart from the normal ones.

I think we are going toward very difficult times. Men and women are going to need a lot of courage to safeguard the dignity of humankind. We are entering a dramatic epoch and what we need is extra wisdom to control our new powers. I am very struck by the parallel between the progress of industry in the nineteenth century and the progress of biology in our times. Industrial progress in the nineteenth century took place at the cost of terrible social upheavals; that is why Marxist theories appeared then. Now the application of biology to the human species is producing terrible human and moral damage. The manipulation of animal species has become quite common. But the basic questions coming up are moral ones: What is the relation of human beings to their bodies? To what extent can they do what they like with their bodies? To what extent can they do what they like with themselves? Human beings may have great powers and be the object of technical experiment, but they are above all morally responsible beings, *subjects:* as such they may not be equated to other objects. Everything may be possible but not everything is right. I cannot help thinking with horror of the experiments which Mengele carried out in Nazi concentration camps. Some of the mad experiments on human beings are going to turn us into the sorcerer's apprentice.

But does all this mean that one may not try to help a woman to have a child when she can't have one?

Is that really where the debate lies? We must face up to a rigorous examination of what being human is. I saw a television interview recently on which a women was saying that she wanted to have children but had just had two abortions. I think that is dreadful. The child has become simply an object to be desired.

Catholic Schools Are Part of Our Inheritance

The bishops of France at their last assembly in Lourdes underlined the visible nature of the Church. The pope has spoken about it too to the bishops of the West and he mentioned Christian schools as part of it. Do you still see this visible character of the Church as requiring institutions today?

Yes, I see institutions as necessary. I don't see how a social reality can exist without institutions. If one wants to solve the school question, one has to widen the debate. It is necessary to see that the relation between parents and children is not just functional; the whole notion of descendants, and therefore of education, involves much more than just supply and demand. We are touching here on the commandment to transmit life which must be obeyed by every community whatever it may be.

It is a commandment of God that life must be handed on. It is also a serious duty to hand on the life of faith by education. Schools are a particularly good way of fulfilling this mission, though they are not the only way.

Catholic schools are places where the Gospel must be proclaimed, welcomed, and handed on. In our situation in France, it is evident that Catholic schools reflect as many different tendencies as do Catholics themselves.

From a more general point of view, Catholic schools with their own educational methods are a part of the inheritance of the French nation. At a time when education is in crisis, I do not see how one could reasonably destroy a part of that inheritance without putting the equilibrium of our whole society seriously in danger. Why should Catholics give up one of their lawful rights which contributes usefully to the common good? All this is so

An interview with Gérard Leclerc in *Le Quotidien,* 10–11 April 1982.

obvious that it fully justifies the firm determination on the part of Christians to maintain as necessary their own special contribution. Certainly the firm and unanimous convictions of the hierarchy are not in doubt. I think that all French citizens have the duty of showing respect and toleration so as not to divide the nation on this issue.

Private Schools and Public Service

What conclusions would you draw from the national demonstration of 24 June with which you were associated?

I think this demonstration, which brought together all those who make up Catholic education, was remarkable by its size, by its good order, and by the fact that it started at the Place de la Bastille.[1] All those who saw it said that it was a national event and, doubtless, something which had never happened before in the history of Paris. As I said at Versailles, none of our political parties could have brought together such a huge crowd of people from so many different backgrounds.

Basically this happening cannot be equated with the normal vicissitudes of politics. The whole organization, which was remarkably well done, and the numbers who came depended on a voluntary team which was very committed and completely unpaid.

This was a free demonstration in favor of freedom. People were manifesting first of all their inner independence in relation to ideologies, clichés, and divisions. So 24 June was first a very enjoyable happening. The atmosphere was that of a popular fiesta. Many commentators remarked that it was like a peaceful version of the demos in May 1968.

There would not have been such an atmosphere of freedom if those taking part had not already experienced it. The way the crowd organized itself in the Place de la Bastille was made possible by the experience of free association in

An interview with François d'Orcival and Yann Clerc, in *Valeurs actuelles*, 2 July 1984.

1. The Place de la Bastille, on the east side of the old city of Paris, occupies the site of the fortress which was stormed by the mob on 14 July 1789, an event which is usually taken as the start of the French Revolution. The Place de la Bastille is traditionally the starting point for republican or left-wing demonstrations. (Translator's note)

private schools which is going on all over France. It would be dangerous to underestimate the strength which is given by such an experience.

The existence of private schools involves all those concerned in a voluntary undertaking of major importance. This applies to all those who are partners in the schools, that is, the parents, the children, the principals, the teachers and educators, the administration, the brothers, the nuns, and the priests. They are all of them involved as a result of the juridical status of the schools, as strengthened by the law of 1959 and subsequent decisions. I call this an undertaking of major importance because it concerns not only the young people and their families but also the vital link between the two which tends to be separated by the way an administration organizes things. The relations between one generation and the next is one of the most sensitive areas in the problems of society. It is an area where the real responsibility of each person comes into play and where the future of a nation is decided.

So it is not surprising that this is an area where free association is especially likely to occur and where voluntary bodies appear which can give to the individual the required scope; here spiritual communities and their solidarity are often found. The more positive aspects of the demo on 24 June gave evidence of a new form of citizenship coming into being; the evidence came in the way each person demonstrated by his or her freedom on behalf of the freedom of all.

That is why I have always considered that this type of community organization of autonomous schools is not only demanded by parents for private schools. If it is a privilege, then it ought to be extended to state schools as well.

Why did you take part only indirectly in the demo? You brought along a message from the bishops but you did not lead the march. What were you afraid of?

I wasn't afraid of anything. Heavens above! Are you joking or something! We bishops are responsible to God. That is much worse than being responsible to human beings, but at least it does free us from acting through fear.

I would like to ask you two questions. First, since the Church asks lay people to assume their responsibilities, would it have been right for the bishops to take over a movement of parents which has its own leaders, already democratically elected? That would have been an example of the obscurantist clericalism which some people still consider as characteristic of Catholics.

What the bishops did was to fulfill their duty as trustees, responsible for the Catholic nature of these schools; they kept to this role by their support and by their constant vigilance. This is what we had to do and what we wanted to do anyway. We were making this clear in word and deed long before 24 June.

My second question concerns the application to the Church of the current models of organizing people. Is it relevant to speak of militants and sympathizers, of charismatic leaders and bureaucratic leaders who either follow or rally their troops? Is there such a thing as a strategy for seizing power, either in the Church or by the Church? Someone who analyzes things this way will eventually be surprised by the way they turn out.

The real unity of the Catholic Church is the possibility given by the Holy Spirit of living in Christ as adopted children of the Father. Everything else is the freedom of the children of God. Christians and others who demonstrated in the Place de la Bastille were using their freedom; they were not driven by what priests told them in the secret of the confessional. The Church does not mobilize her battalions; she invites people to communion and to an exercise of freedom in its various forms.

Do you think that the public image of the Church in France has been changed as a result of the demo?

I want to air a theory. Since the age of the Enlightenment, the Church has been constantly accused of demeaning human beings as regards the exercise of their rights, whatever it said about their nature. For over three centuries, these accusations have been repeated over and over again, and drummed into people.

Now the Church has become one of the last bastions for the defense of humankind, as the result of all sorts of historical and intellectual reasons; one of these is the disappearance of the idea that humankind can supply all its needs and be totally independent. That idea was studied by Michel Foucault who has just died.[2] But now we see human beings as the subjects of certain rights. Christians believe this because they believe in God and because they believe in Christ. They receive the Spirit of Christ so as to be witnesses to him, even at the cost of martyrdom.

It is clear that the Church claims these rights for humankind without conditions or qualifications. It claims them, whatever the political regime may be and for all parts of the earth, from Poland to Chile and from Nicaragua to Korea. Everywhere the Church asks that the rights of unborn children may be respected, that millions of human beings be saved from death by starvation, that persecutions in the name of religion may cease, and that the rights of immigrants may be recognized.

One can blame the Church and Christians for all sorts of things but not for keeping silent over human rights. Because the faith frees them from ideologies, Christians are able to plead for the dignity of humankind, created in the image and likeness of God, as much as anybody else and sometimes more than others.

In the case of France, Christians were not just defending their own interests. They were the peaceful affirmers of rights which are common to all

2. Michel Foucault (1926–84) was a French philosopher and historian, who at the time of his death held the chair of the History of Systems of Thought at the College de France. His best known work is *The Order of Things*. (Translator's note)

citizens. From now it is evident to all French persons that the Church defends human rights because it respects the rights of God. Christians know it now.

Do you think that the school question is going to come up again and again, now that M. Mauroy has spread out over eleven years the implementation of the Savory reform of education, including EIPs, tenure, finances, and the reform of the law?[3]

If this were to happen and if the school question were to become a school war, then France would suffer the sort of national catastrophe that we have always tried to avoid. Let us hope that nothing of the sort happens. What the government should do is review its project for legislation and negotiate again on the contested points, some of which were the result of last-minute amendments; or else it should take note of the work that the Senate is due to do on the bill.

Otherwise I am afraid that the government will be exposed to a fierce reaction from those responsible for Catholic schools. But surely a left-wing administration should recognize a popular movement when it sees one and I do not doubt that it will. But in any case it is necessary, and urgently so, that the restructuring of the educational system should apply to private schools as well.

Why is that?

I am convinced that private schools are playing an important part within the French system of education. If I were minister of National Education, I would think twice before disturbing the links which have grown up between the various types of schools which together make up our national education system. It could well be that within this plurality lies the possibility of the innovations that we need to face the challenge which young people constitute for the country.

3. In 1982–83 the Socialist government of Prime Minister Pierre Mauroy and Education Minister Alain Savary tried to keep the promises made by President François Mitterrand during his election campaign to nationalize all private schools in receipt of government grants; 90 percent of these were Catholic schools. The government proposal was to transform them into EIPs *(Etablissements d'Intérêt Public)* under government control. This proposal satisfied no one since many Socialists considered that it was not genuine nationalization, while Catholic parents wanted to maintain the independence of the schools. Representatives of the schools and the parents negotiated with the government and reached a compromise with proposals for GPIEs *(Groupements Publics d'Intérêt Educatif)*, but Socialist hard-liners amended the bill and this triggered a series of mass demonstrations. The largest was in Paris at the Place de la Bastille on 24 June 1984 and brought together over two million demonstrators. Savary and Mauroy resigned and President Mitterrand announced on 12 July that the bill was withdrawn. Cardinal Lustiger's interview in *Le Monde*, 5 June 1984 (not reproduced here), and this interview with *Valeurs actuelles* are considered decisive in their influence on public opinion which led to the president's change of policy. (Translator's note)

But, even if you are not the minister of National Education, you are still the archbishop of Paris.

Yes, the real question today is to find out how a Catholic school can be worthy of the name. This is what I said in all the public statements I have made on the question. When I was bishop of Orleans, I was invited to give a talk to a training session for teachers in private schools. This is more or less what I said: "My real worry about Catholic schools is that they should be really Catholic. What is needed for this is that teachers and all those responsible for the school should be deeply concerned to become ever more truly Catholic themselves."

The quality of religious education depends primarily on the clarity and the coherence of teachers in their role as witnesses to the faith; statutory guarantees for the Catholic school are necessary but they are secondary. Many attitudes are beginning to change in that respect.

What young people, and especially young married couples who are concerned for the religious education of their children, are doing is preparing new ways of having Catholic schools. They are going to invent new types of schools to suit them. In a secularized society one will be compelled to be really committed to the religious aspect of education.

What is the strategy of the Church? Does it want to ensure a Christian education or to prevent a monolithic system of education?

When you are claiming a fundamental freedom in matters of education, you are not dealing in strategies or opportunism; you are proclaiming a right. Among our basic freedoms should be listed the freedom of the individual and the right of parents to transmit to their children the fundamental values, including the religious values, that they believe in. It should be possible to exercise this right within the educational system. This prevents the totalitarian control of education by the state, which is a possibility even in a democratic state.

Having said this, the Church has always recognized that the state, the Church (in the case of those who call themselves Christian), and families each have rights where education is concerned. These three are partners in education and should respect their mutual area of competence and responsibility.

Insofar as a child or a young person is also a citizen, it is normal that the state should guarantee the values of the nation and should intervene if necessary to guarantee the rights of families and the right of freedom of religious education. It is not enough for the state not to thwart these rights; it must also guarantee practical conditions for their exercise.

That is the question. Where are the priorities in the present debate?

For over half a century French Catholics have been campaigning for a recognition of their place within the state system of education and for a respect for their rights.

What exactly does the idea of *laïcité* imply? Is it a positivist, antireligious ideal, as at the beginning of this century? Or is it a certain neutrality which respects consciences and would allow believers too to have their lawful place within the state system of education, without persecution or suspicion because of their faith?

There has been progress in this matter but it has been extremely slow. Thus it was only after the Second World War that it was tolerated in higher education that a professor could state publicly that he or she was a believer, either Catholic, Protestant, or Jewish. Then the same thing became accepted in state secondary schools and finally, though with the greatest difficulty of all, in state primary schools.

This liberalization became possible because of the intellectual evolution which occurred in the years after the Second World War. From the point of view of pupils, it gradually became acceptable for Catholics to send their children to state schools and for the values of religious education to be given otherwise than in a Catholic school.

So if we are defending today the special character of Catholic schools, we must be careful not to disallow or prevent the work of those who are devoting themselves to the religious education of children within state schools. We must also appreciate the teachers in these schools who respect the conscientiously held beliefs of the children whom they instruct.

The real need is to come to a clear idea of what religious education can be in a pluralistic society on the way to secularization. Catholics have the responsibility of working for the safeguard of people's liberty; we have to guarantee suitable ways of exercising that liberty in education. But, when all this has been done, we still have to ask ourselves the question: "Now that we have the required legal framework, have we found the means of giving a specifically Christian education?" It would be quite possible to win the legal safeguards and then to fail to achieve what is allowed by them.

Do you think that this great movement to save Catholic schools and find new ways of teaching the faith is perhaps creating a false impression that most of the French are Catholics, whereas Catholics are really a minority?

Every twenty years or so, the most outstanding men and women of their generation rediscover for themselves the requirements of a lively faith. They are naturally a spiritual minority, but in realizing the fact they discover ways of surviving in a state of mild nonconformity. This was already so in the days of Saint Francis of Assisi and Saint Vincent de Paul. A really living faith needs a certain solitude in order to find the way to survive.

The Christian faith is such that it does not find its fulfillment in becoming the religious culture for a given period of civilization. What it must do is to proclaim anew for each individual and for each generation the call to conversion in the steps of Christ and through his Passion.

CHURCH AND STATE

※

Give Back to Caesar
What Belongs to Caesar

Matt. 22:15–21

A re you aware of the implications of those striking words of Jesus? No doubt you are; nevertheless I am going to remind you of what they mean. Many are the commentators who see in this text the basis for an equitable division of the empire of the world between Caesar and God. The question of the sharing of power, both in the temporal and in the spiritual sphere, is a real question about a real issue. But no argument about it can be based on these words of Christ.

What does Jesus mean? A trap has been laid for him; it is a trial, or a temptation as Matthew calls it. Jesus' reaction is to refer indirectly to the commandment given to Israel: everything belongs to God, he only has the fullness of power over his people, he alone is the true king of the nation. So, far from justifying a sharing of powers or dominion, the words of Jesus indicate the opposite. "What belongs to Caesar must be given back to Caesar" because his effigy is stamped in this money. Caesar is only the owner of *this coin here,* which is a means given by Caesar for dealing with the affairs of Caesar. But by contrast, "giving back to God what belongs to God" means for the chosen people remembering that it is made for God, that it belongs completely to God, and that everything belongs to God. The first commandment is: "Thou shalt love the Lord thy God with thy whole strength and with thy whole soul and above all things." And the second is like unto it: "Thou shalt love thy neighbor as thyself."

Jesus' answer gives rise to another difficulty which is easy to see in the

A meditation for Catholic lawyers, assembled at the Cathedral of Notre-Dame de Paris, 12 November 1982.

context of the Roman Empire: Caesar was trying to take the place of God. The central area where a human society finds its unity is a place which is symbolically sacred and which enjoys a divine investiture. It is a focal point for all the sacred elements and for the cohesion of society, where its ambitions are made manifest, a quasi-divine location. Who is to occupy it? In this debate and this conflict, is it Caesar who becomes God or God who becomes Caesar? What is at stake here is the whole question of power and politics, a fascinating subject with religious overtones.

What Jesus is saying is that God alone is God and that no thing or person in the world should lay claim to be God or to usurp his place. Humankind's supreme dignity lies in the fact that it is called to acknowledge that God alone is God and in the fact that it can adore God. Because of the respect due to human dignity, there should not be any sharing or compromise between God and Caesar, as if they were in competition. There can be no agreement between God and Caesar in the way the powers of this world, two powers within the same society, can legitimately balance each other, compensate each other, reach an agreement and, by means of legal agreement and negotiation, find the means for coexistence and cooperation. God and Caesar cannot reach such a compromise because it would inevitably lead to a betrayal of what God is, God who is the only God; or it would be a betrayal of what humankind is by making it the slave of one man or woman.

As I have said, this saying of Jesus is mistakenly used to solve the relations of Church and state, whereas these depend on an entirely different question. This is another area altogether. The Church has never claimed that it is God, any more than it can claim to be Christ. The Church is the body of Christ and the temple of the Holy Spirit, but it is not the one whom it worships nor the one who dwells in it. The Church is not the one whom it proclaims, even though the one whom it receives makes it like him. It is not God, even though the divinization of humanity occurs within it by grace. It is not the kingdom of God, even though it shows the kingdom forth and announces it.

There is a constant gap between two realities. One is already given as a real firstfruits of the gift of grace and anticipates the kingdom that is to come; it is a prophecy of what is revealed in the Book of the Apocalypse as the fulfillment of all things in humanity, when all people will be brought together in a communion of holiness without shadows and a redemption finally achieved. The other reality is the Church still on its pilgrim way, the humble sign of the first reality and a sign which is constantly being humiliated by the sins of its members. And yet the one and only Church is the temple of the one who was crucified; there he shares his Resurrection when he gives himself as the Bread of Life; there he becomes the source of life for a sinful world so that the world too can enter into glory.

The Church itself, or rather people within the Church, can be tempted, like Caesar, to put themselves in the place of the one whom they are proclaiming.

They can be tempted by power as Caesar is, especially by the sacred character of power. This is one of the temptations of Christ in the desert which foretold the temptations that we would have to overcome: Satan took Christ to the pinnacle of the temple and said: "If you are the Son of God, throw yourself down" (Matt. 4:5–6). For the Son that would have meant usurping the authority of the Father. It would have meant misusing the gift of grace and mercy given in the very temple. The Church and its members also can be tempted to behave like the princes of this world who like to be called benefactors.

Do you remember the argument which took place among the apostles before the Passion about who should be called the greatest? Christ said to them: "the kings of the Gentiles exercise Lordship over them and those in authority over them are called benefactors," but Jesus commands them: "not so with you; rather let the greatest among you become as the youngest and the leader as one who serves . . . I am among you as one who serves" (Luke 22:25–27). Already Jesus had told the sons of Zebedee: "the Son of Man came not to be served but to serve and to give his life as a ransom for many" (Mark 10:45). This temptation was felt by the apostles; it is also felt by those to whom the Church gives authority and who are its foundation stones, in spite of their weakness. But Jesus has promised to give them the strength of the Spirit to overcome it. In this way will they be identified with their crucified Lord who became a servant to redeem the sin of humanity.

It is understandable that throughout the centuries the relations between the civil power and the religious power should have been expressed in different forms, according to time and place. This relationship has never been something unproblematic and serene; it has always been a source of temptation and trial. Human power has a fascination about it which can lead humanity to put itself in the place of the absolute, which is God. As for the Church, it can rightly say that it is a disinterested servant, recognizing the normal sovereignty of the civil power and only desirous of being at the service of humankind. When it does that, it is not basely submitting to a power which alienates humankind; what it is doing is exercising clearly the sovereign liberty which God gives into its care.

When one is trying to understand this saying of Christ: "Give back to Caesar what belongs to Caesar and to God what belongs to God," one should remember how the apostles who first heard it came to put it into practice. They were dragged before a court which forbade them to preach in the name of Christ and they said: "It is better to obey God than man." This supreme freedom comes from a complete obedience given to God, even to the point of martyrdom. Then and only then can the Church appear not as a power in competition with others, defending its jurisdiction over and against other jurisdictions. In varied forms and in strange situations, the Church is revealed as giving a service of love which is a gift of oneself and an identification with the crucified Christ. This is a reminder in the midst of this confused and changing world that God is the absolute and the basis of humankind's true freedom.

The rights of the Church and its sovereignty are the same thing basically as the fact that it must obey God and not human creatures. It is never more sovereign than when it obeys its only Lord. When the Church is obedient to God, then it can be a servant with the Servant of God. This is a paradox and a situation which is always misunderstood or not understood at all. Christians are always suspected of hiding under these fine words, which are not really understood, some perverse attempt at self-interest; as if we were trying to recuperate some fragment of worldly power for our own profit and ends. And it must be admitted that there is a real temptation. The Church must ceaselessly give evidence of its sincerity by letting its fidelity be put to the test. All the time it must be prepared to give a fundamental witness; it does this by showing forth the power of God even when it appears to be heading for crucifixion and defeat. The history of past centuries demonstrates to the eyes of faith and with hindsight that God's power is revealed in our weakness and that the victory of the Church is based on the strength of the martyrs and of love.

Perhaps this meditation has been too theological; your concerns are more practical and rightly so. But I hope that what I have said may provide a background for understanding the liberty of the Church and its freedom to read and discern events and situations. This is the same freedom as the apostles had; they were given as a sight to the world and handed over into human power with the Son as a supreme sign of God's love.

In these times we are experiencing in many countries great uncertainty about the future of basic rights. This is why it is so necessary to safeguard what is essential to humanity, even though humankind may be tempted to forget it and to disregard its own dignity. So it is the duty of Christians to go as far as possible in obedience to God so that thus humanity can be saved; this is our vocation and the grace we can bring.

May God give to all of you and to each of us the grace to follow the master on this path with the complete generosity of disciples and with the joy which comes from experiencing the freedom of the sons and daughters of God who are exempt from the toll and tribute exacted by the kings of the earth (cf. Matt. 17:25–26). Thus will you be able to witness to the liberty of the children of God which is the basis of all rights.

The Church and Politics

*D*o *you think that the Church has a role to play in politics?*

I don't want to pronounce on an open question so I will keep to the essentials. Yes, of course the Church has a role to play in politics, though in varied ways. First of all, it has a political role in ensuring its own existence within society. This concrete existence based on freedom of worship implies concrete rights. For example, the Church claims the right and the means to educate in a Christian way the young people who are the children of its children. I have already had the opportunity of explaining publicly what this spiritual right involves in terms of social life.[1] The Church also has the right of making public statements and so can be exempt from the monopoly imposed on the media.

The Church also plays a political role when it has the courage to say what are the political consequences of the spiritual demands contained in the Gospel. For instance, once it is accepted that human beings are defined as the image and likeness of God, then the Church must require the state not to treat them like animals. Hence the Church condemns certain genetic manipulations, euthanasia, and abortion. The Church defends the right to work, social justice, and the integration into society of all those who have been excluded from it. When liberty is being mocked, the Church defends the rights of ordinary citizens. In very many cases what the Church says expresses the silent aspirations of the majority and those in power give it positive backing.

However, I think that at present what the Church says is going to have a threefold political impact, corresponding to the three most dramatic questions of our times. Since our nation is faced with an economic crisis which is tearing society apart, it is the Church which can give powerful support to

An interview with Jean Bourdarias, in *Le Figaro*, 28 September 1982.

1. See the section "Youth and School" in this book. (Translator's note)

119

efforts to maintain the unity of our society; it can do this by helping people to avoid a purely selfish reaction to the crisis according to their class interest; it can help people to adopt a new lifestyle.[2]

Then there is the question of terrorism. Of course the Church condemns it, wherever it comes from. Not every country will do this, or can do it. The Church above all can strengthen the resolve not to give in to the pressure of terrorism; one must not go down to its level under pretext of fighting against it. One must put one's trust in intelligence, strength, and forgiveness. These are the cardinal virtues of yesterday, of which the theologians used to speak.

Finally, there are the suicidal war games between nations and states, for example, in the Middle East. The Church can sometimes be more effective than politicians in bringing about reconciliation, mutual recognition, and peace; when people are crazed through terror and fear, they don't believe in these anymore. Without ever entering directly into politics, the Church must fulfill its task which is a spiritual one. But a spiritual task is above all a real task.

Everything spiritual is real; that is really my message to you.

2. On 22 September 1982 the Standing Committee of the French bishops issued a statement on new lifestyles entitled "Pour de nouveaux modes de vie." (Translator's note)

The Transcendence of Love

*I*t *is obvious that the Church is on the side of popular feeling on the school
question. But this was not so for abortion. Why the difference?*

I have noted an alarming fact; in the space of one year, if the Gallup polls
are to be trusted, the moral and social judgment of the French people veered
from one position to its exact opposite. Don't you think it strange that moral
attitudes could thus do a U-turn? What can one make of such a sudden
change? Can one change the way conscience works as one changes a one-way
system?

What this change of attitude indicates is that abortion was already being
seen as a morally indifferent act. People disapproved of it because of social
habits of thought and behavior or else because of class attitudes. But the issue
is really a much deeper one and concerns the respect of human conscience
enlightened by faith for life as given by God to a human person. What this
sudden U-turn in morality indicates is that the French had no moral conviction on the matter, or else that it was very weak, or that it was merely a matter
of convention. All of which is very worrying.

*One gets the impression that in the collective subconscious of the French people
Church and state have always been seen as one.*

What happened in France was that the state had to impose unity and
central government on the country. The Church was very tempted, since it
did not always have the support of the people, to try to influence the political
center of power in order to guarantee its mission. On the other hand, the
state has always tried to control the Church as a means of ensuring its
predominance.

In other words, political power in France has always been fascinated by the
sacred, and the sacred has always been fascinated by political power. In

An interview with François d'Orcival and Yann Clerc, in *Valeurs actuelles*, 2 July
1984.

121

France more than in other countries, political conflicts were often wars of religion and the wars of religion were often political conflicts.

What do you think should be said to Christians?

That one is a Christian by God's grace and not as of right. One is *chosen* as the Scriptures say. A Christian should know about two basic things, God's choice and the Church's mission, so he or she sees the Church as a gift of grace and his or her baptism as a calling.

The way in which Christianity ceaselessly renews itself is always a cause of surprise for modern unbelievers; they identify progress with the inevitable decay of religion. It is only if you accept unconsciously the theory that a secularized society is inevitable that you cannot understand the religious revival. Such people are very surprised to see that reality is not at all what they think and that we are basically religious animals, so that our relation to God is part of our nature and our history. Theoretical atheism as produced by the West is one of the major heresies or idolatries of the Christian West.

Is the unity of the Church still under threat in France?

Not at all; at least not if Catholics know how to resist making the Church into an instrument of something else. Sometimes there is a temptation to use the Church as a means or an instrument for some purpose which is outside the Church or even opposed to it. Christians and the bishops are then seen primarily as potential voters, a pressure group, a market, and so on.

This attitude is not surprising on the part of those who are used to seeing everything in terms of political power. But it would be surprising and even shocking on the part of a Christian. I often hear the Church, and especially bishops, criticized by right-wingers and left-wingers because it does not take part in the political warfare which dominates the French scene. I note how constant the attempts are, from whatever side, to separate the faithful from their bishops. There are always plenty of self-appointed "prophets" who think that the only qualification needed is to insult others or, if they are not good at controversy, to blacken their reputation!

All this is a complete misunderstanding of the level at which the Church operates. The Church does not take part in the pitiless confrontation of different ideologies and their struggle for power. What the Church seeks is the lowliness which comes from love; this implies the love of one's enemies, the forgiveness of offenses, and mercy for others. In the political debate, on the other hand, love appears to be weakness and even treason if it persists. So the Church, and especially bishops, are bound to be suspect, rightly or wrongly, to both the right and the left.

What I would like to ask Catholics and others is this: If the Church is a sign of contradiction at the political level, is this not because love must inevitably transcend every other reality? If that is so, then they must respect love, even if they do not practice it.

The Church of France will have been through a time of great trial. Do you think that the school question will have helped it to overcome?

I am very struck by the fact that the problems of the Church of France are not peculiar to the Church of France. They are part of the crisis of the West and its spoiled children (in every sense of the word).

We must overcome this trial. No one is going to do it for us. If we manage it, we shall be contributing to the salvation of other continents and other cultures.

Whether we like it or not, technology has taken a universal hold; this is a fact. Humankind has to come to terms with reason. Even the human body has become the object of amazing control by science; this can lead to abuse but it can also be a cause of progress.

What is needed is that those who wield such power should somehow be converted. There has to be a conversion in depth if humanity is not to lose itself during the course of its history. Those who have a role in modern culture must become the reformers of that culture. Salvation always comes in times of crisis. "Where the danger is greatest, there is the savior to be found" (Hölderlin).

The Duty of the Churches

My Lord Archbishop:

It is with a very special joy that the archbishop of Paris welcomes to this cathedral the primate of all England and the first bishop of the whole Anglican communion. We are not only linked by a past which goes back to Saint Augustine of Canterbury and to the long history which our two Christian countries have had in common. Since the historic meeting which took place in 1966 between Pope Paul VI and your predecessor, Dr. Ramsey, there have been warm and constant exchanges in prayer and brotherly charity between the archbishop of Paris and the archbishop of Canterbury. Already on 22 April 1967 Archbishop Veuillot gave a solemn welcome to Dr. Ramsey in this very place. Since then Cardinal Marty has never ceased to maintain this tradition and to deepen it with Dr. Ramsey, Dr. Coggan, and yourself; the words which you have just spoken will strengthen those links, update them, and make them more fruitful.

It is with deep interest that I listened to Your Grace's meditation on the twin destiny of our two countries and our two churches. While following such a line of thought and the vistas which it opens up, I found that other differences and other similarities came to my mind.

First, the history of our two countries is perhaps more different than appears at first sight. I am thinking of the fact that the English language, deriving from Anglo-Saxon and Norman origins, reached its maturity with the Authorized Version of the Bible which marked the end of a century of deep crisis and the entry into the modern world. The Word of God in the Old and New Testament thus formed your language and therefore your culture. On the contrary, one can say of the French language that it was formed by the gods of classical antiquity which the Renaissance brought back into fashion

A reply to the speech by Dr. Runcie, archbishop of Canterbury, at the Cathedral of Notre-Dame de Paris, 2 December 1984.

without bringing them back to life. Thus a triumphant paganism provided part of the background for modern French culture.

If one wants proof of this difference, one has only to compare two of our foundation documents, both published in 1549. In your case it was the first edition of the famous *Book of Common Prayer* which expressed a national unity both of language and religion. In our case it was the *Défense et illustration de la langue française*, equally famous but with nothing specifically Christian about it. In it Du Bellay and his friends (a group called *la Brigade* who were to become *la Pléiade*) argued that salvation lay in rejecting not only the forms but also the subjects and themes of the Middle Ages. Classical antiquity must be imitated:

> O future poet, make it your first duty to read over and over again, to turn over by day and by night the pages of Greek and Latin literature; put aside all those old French poems. . . . Sing the odes as yet unknown of the Gallic Muse; tune your lute to the sound of the lyre of the Greeks and the Romans. Let there be no verse without some trace of a rare and antique erudition.

Obviously classical antiquity influenced English literature too, from the Renaissance to the Augustan age and beyond. But it did not have the same preponderance or exercise the same domination as in French culture. From Chaucer to Milton by way of Shakespeare, what one sees is the creation of a national identity based on a language and a view of the world derived from the Bible and the Christian faith.

One could object that it was the Reformation which produced in the case of England an immediate merging of nation, language, and biblical tradition, whereas France received its identity and its language from paganism as much as from Christianity so that the Latin which influenced French was classical Latin and not the Latin of the Church. However, one should take note of the fact that the identity of nation and religion which are characteristic of England also occur in other European nations, but without the identification of the Reformation with their linguistic unity. This happened in several Central European countries and in nations of the Eastern Marches; they managed to combine fidelity to Rome with a vigorous consciousness of their cultural and national identity. The best example of this is Poland, which you yourself have just mentioned.

Returning to the comparison between our two countries, I would say that you were born as Christians whereas we were partially born as pagans. That is the first difference.

I will now go further and venture to give a cursory account of our history which will no doubt send shivers down the spine of some of the academics who dwell on the banks of the river Seine. I hope that those who wander peacefully around the Thames will take it more lightheartedly.

The religious history of England is largely coterminous with that of an

Established Church. One could of course say the same thing about the Catholic Church in France, at least until the revolutionary era. But in the British Isles Christianity also received the stamp of the Reformation. This was one more difference from French Catholicism; but it also produced a Church which was unique and different from all the other churches separated from Rome but not "Established" in the same way.

The Church of England has been deeply influenced by a certain number of spiritual renewals, awakenings, and revivals. Sometimes these movements led to divisions if not to complete breaks. A similar phenomenon was often to be seen in other churches issuing from the Reformation. But elsewhere these divisions were not felt so deeply insofar as churches were not the guardian of national unity; nor did they practice the pluralism and the moderation which the judicious Hooker calls *comprehensiveness* and which Newman when young acclaimed as the *via media* of Anglicanism.

In France too there have been spiritual revival movements since the seventeenth century. But it seems that most of these French revivals found their place within the unity of the Catholic Church; they led to the formation of new religious congregations and also to lay movements. Each of these movements gave new vigor to one or other aspect of Catholic spirituality; they thus enriched our "Established" Church with a whole range of "spiritualities"; they led it to deepen its identity and its tradition while renewing itself.

On your side of the channel, however, it seems that all the new discoveries and insights could not be integrated into the Established Church so that its comprehensiveness began to fail. Can one still say that pragmatism is only to be found on the Anglican side? The Church of England has seen a succession of reformers leave, whereas the Catholic Church has perhaps more often given them recognition and welcomed them as further resources for its own renewal.

I wonder too if the tendency to produce theoretical systems of thought, which is considered usually and perhaps wrongly as an exclusive characteristic of Cartesian logic and of the French mind, is really unknown in Great Britain.

I am alluding here to the relations between Church and state in our two countries. Those who are not English find it difficult to see how national unity can be institutionally linked to the Established Church when they see the extraordinary cultural, philosophical, and ethnic diversity in your country. All the elements of a sacred society are still there and they prop up the civil side of national life; but at the same time there is a secularization of which you have emphasized the extent. So there is a growing gap between the theory and the reality. This must be a cause for concern both because it is relatively new and because it threatens the very foundation of your country.

On the other hand, secularism is much more a part of our inheritance. I have alluded to the pagan influences on the French language and French culture during the sixteenth century. One should add that it is very probable that France was never converted to Christianity in depth. Even the religious unity of the Middle Ages, which cannot be denied at the formal exterior level, should not deceive us. Denis de Rougemont had already shown in 1938 in his masterly study *Love in the Western World* that there was a disturbing connection between the troubadour literature of the Middle Ages, where our culture has its roots (whatever Du Bellay and his friends may have said), and the paganism which arose in the south of France with the Cathars, just at the time when France became one country and was theoretically Christian.

Denis de Rougemont calls passionate love "one of the side-effects of Christianity . . . on minds where a natural or inherited paganism still lived on." He calls it "a historically determined Christian heresy" and says that "our great literatures are to a large extent a laicization of the myth . . . or successive profanations of its content and its form." Thus already in the Middle Ages, before the French language received its form and its inspiration at the Renaissance under the influence of classical antiquity, there was a pagan substratum to French culture. It was in France too that the Albigensian heresy developed.

True there were in England, as in other European countries, heretical movements such as the Lollards. But one must admit that they were not nearly as radical as the Cathars in the south of France. The religious history of France is thus marked by a succession of evangelizations and re-evangelizations. France has always needed "internal missions," as it still does today. If France had ever been thoroughly Christian, there would have been no need for such missions, but in fact they had to be undertaken over and over again, by religious orders especially founded for this purpose and by saints who are renowned for their achievements in this field, Saint Vincent Ferrer in the Middle Ages, Saint Vincent de Paul in the seventeenth century, and the Curé d'Ars in the nineteenth. We should not forget that those parts of France which are considered as traditionally Catholic today have only been so for three hundred years or less.

It is also necessary to underline the complexity of Church-state relations in France throughout history. Louis IX may have been canonized but his grandson Philip IV, known as Philip the Fair, came into violent conflict with the Holy See. It was his legal experts who based themselves on ancient Roman law to perfect the theory of the independence of the state in relation to spiritual and religious power. Gallicanism already contains the temptation and the seeds of secularization.

The Church of France found it difficult to pursue and to take up anew its mission of evangelization and to identify with the French nation when kings were in a state of conflict with Rome. Nearly always the Church sided with the political power; this was at a time when the crown was trying to unify and centralize France by bringing together under its authority different populations and cultures and even different regional languages. The Church of France obtained a privileged position within the state as a means of identification with the French nation. But in return the state tended to control the Church so as to confer a religious sanction on its own power over an amalgam which started off without much unity or coherence.

Thus the relation between Church and state in France has always involved passionate conflict, whereas in England on the whole the relation seems to have been more stable and serene. There have been tensions as in the case of the martyrdom of Saint Thomas Becket. But it illustrates my point that in this case the king of England was compelled to do penance, whereas in France Philip the Fair came out of the sad Anagni episode with impunity, even though his victim was not the first archbishop of the kingdom but the pope himself. The reason for the difference is that the king of France based his power on laws which had already been secularized, whereas in England the king could not rule without the Church since the faith was an essential part of the identity of the nation. But this identification meant that one day communion with Rome came to seem no longer necessary.

This can help to explain why later on your king Henry VIII sent Saint Thomas More to the scaffold and said more or less "I am the Church." Louis XIV on the other hand, during another Gallican crisis one hundred and fifty years later, could only say "I am the State." Although he bore the title of "Most Christian King," he could not claim to be the head of the Church of France, although he would have liked to very much. In contrast, the kings of England from Henry VIII to your beloved queen today have had the headship of the Church of England. Louis XIV could not say "I am the Church" because secularization occurred in France far earlier than in England.

Another sequence of apparently very similar and contemporary events in the history of our two countries can serve to illustrate how different our situations are when we are faced with the challenge of secularization. In France Henry of Navarre accepted the established religion and became a Catholic in order to reign as Henry IV; in England James VII of Scotland accepted to become an Anglican so as to become James I of England. But the Edict of Nantes which Henry IV conceded to his former coreligionists set up a "state within a state," whereas James I became the sovereign of a United Kingdom which still survives.

Two generations later, this basic difference came to the fore. Louis XIV, the grandson of Henry IV, revoked the Edict of Nantes in a renewed and unsuccessful attempt to use religion as a means of consolidating national unity. At almost the same time James II, grandson of James I, provoked your Glorious Revolution; it occurred one hundred years before the French Revolution and was totally different. James II tried to reestablish Roman Catholicism, an attempt which was seen by Englishmen of that time as a threat to the sacred character of their institutions and to their national unity.

Since then, however, the presence of an ever-growing number of Roman Catholics in Great Britain has never been a threat to the existence of the United Kingdom. At the beginning of the nineteenth century they recovered all their religious and civil liberties so that the famous passage of the Epistle to Diognetus, which you have just quoted,[1] can very aptly be applied to them. We French Catholics cannot forget the way in which many congregations of religious found a refuge in Great Britain eighty years ago at the worst time of the conflict between Church and state in France.

The history of the sixteenth and seventeenth centuries in your country goes a long way toward explaining how it avoided the bloody revolutions and the rampant secularism which marked the rest of Europe and much of the world since the end of the eighteenth century. Your Church is faced with dechristianization now, but it has maintained in your ancient universities a certain tradition of faith. This has been so in spite of the tide of critical and liberal rationalism flowing from Germany, so that paradoxically it is an estuary which has brought the ground swell to a halt.

This is particularly evident in the field of patristic studies at Oxford (apologies to those from Cambridge) and in the field of exegesis at Cambridge (I apologize to those from Oxford for mentioning Lightfoot, Westcott and Hort, and, nearer to our time, Lord Ramsey and Bishop Robinson). I should also mention the contribution of C. H. Dodd and the outstanding defense of Christianity by C. S. Lewis. All this constitutes a great enrichment for the common future of the Anglican and Roman Catholic churches.

The existence of a common future for these churches is all the surer for the fact that in the past the bridges were never completely down and the tunnel was never completely blocked (even though oddly we are still talking about digging the tunnel today!). The facts and the names have been frequently recalled by our predecessors and I will not repeat them now. I will only recall one particular aspect of those relations which is fundamental by quoting a few examples which may have been overlooked.

At the level of spiritual life, mutual influence never ceased. Thus one cannot but be impressed by the undoubted relationship between Bérulle's theory of the permanent states of Christ (as opposed to his actions in the

---

1. "Christians . . . do not dwell in cities in some place of their own, nor do they use any strange variety of dialect . . . they follow local customs, both in clothing and food and in the rest of life. . . . They dwell in their own fatherlands, but as if foreigners in them; they share all things as citizens and suffer all things as foreigners. Every foreign country is their fatherland and every fatherland is a foreign country. . . . They obey the appointed laws and they surpass the laws in their own lives. . . . To put it shortly what the soul is in the body, that the Christians are in the world" ("The Epistle to Diognetus," V, i–vi, 1, in *The Apostolic Fathers,* edited by Kirksopp Lake [London: William Heinemann, 1913], II:358–60).

past) and a little treatise entitled "The Tender Dispositions of the Heart of Christ in Heaven towards Sinners upon Earth." This was written by Thomas Goodwin more than twenty years before the revelations of Saint Margaret Mary Alacoque. Goodwin was one of the theologians assembled by Cromwell to draw up a new constitution for the Church of England. He was one of the five Dissenting Brethren who founded Congregationalism. It is amusing to discover that this radical Puritan, who disapproved of "Roman" tendencies in the Established Church, was, no doubt unconsciously, very close to the cardinal who founded the French Oratory and to the devotion to the Sacred Heart at Paray-le-Monial.

I will also allude to the way in which Fénelon's ideas on mystical prayer were widely diffused among Methodists at the instigation of Wesley himself, as were the writings of the Carmelite brother from Paris, Laurence of the Resurrection. Finally, I will mention briefly the influence on Christians in France of the antislavery movement of William Wilberforce and the social Christianity of Frederick Dennison Maurice (who seems incidentally to have been the inventor of the term *Anglicanism.*)

Maurice and Wilberforce, among many others, campaigned for human rights, and this brings me to the worldwide dimensions of the Anglican communion. Its symbol is perhaps Bishop Desmond Tutu who is due to receive in a few days' time the Nobel Peace Prize. This outstanding black bishop from South Africa is typically Anglican in not basing on human reason his opposition to the institutionalism of racism which is *apartheid;* he bases his political stance on faith and denounces *apartheid* as a heresy, while preaching reconciliation and a "civilization of love," a phrase already used by Pope Paul VI.

There thus exist many reasons for convergence, confidence, and even admiration between our two communions; they can see the way ahead though not without obstacles. One of these which is bound to cause us alarm is a recent decision of the Synod of the Church of England on the ordination of women to the priesthood. If this decision were to be put into effect it could cause an almost complete breach, not only with the Catholic Church but also with the Orthodox and within Anglicanism itself. In 1975 Pope Paul VI had already clearly stated in his letter to your predecessor Dr. Coggan: "the ordination of women cannot be accepted for absolutely fundamental reasons." What is at stake here is nothing less than the way we must follow.

However, I want to express hearty approval of the four signposts which you have just indicated.[2] Allow me to add though that there is a sign in heaven for those who are traveling; I hope this will not distract them from

---

2. Dr. Runcie had mentioned four signposts which indicate the real nature of a community: family virtues, ascetic practices, loyalty, and prophetic vision.

their road. The vision which you have identified could appear as still marked with a Christian identity which derives from secular institutions. But the hope which I sensed in your speech risks being put to the test of secularization, as we have been ourselves. In other words, is humanism enough, even though it has a Christian inspiration, as an answer to the formidable questions asked by Marx, Nietzsche, and Freud? These masters of modern thought, who have been dubbed by Paul Ricoeur "the masters of suspicion," have ushered in a modern era in which it seems that the triumph of reason can only be at the expense of the faith. But reason has turned out to be totalitarian and imperialist; today we can see humankind in danger of destroying itself because it is no longer certain about the existence of a human condition which is worthy of being respected and loved. Only the faith therefore can save humankind by its affirmation that it is of God and comes from God. In our secularized societies, the question of God has become the major problem because it is the basis for resolving the question of humanity.

Being modern is not incompatible with being a believer, as people tended to think in the nineteenth century. Secularism itself is the product of Christianity. Without Christianity, secularism cannot be understood. Rationalism and the power of humankind over itself and its environment are the product of faith. Whether one likes it or not, it is faith which has elevated reason. It is the Christian view of the world as something given by God to humankind which has made the progress of the sciences and of technology possible.

But God's gifts can be perverted if we attempt to appropriate them and to monopolize them. The results are then both suicidal and homicidal. We are discovering this in the twentieth century with abortion, the refusal to transmit life, genetic engineering, totalitarian regimes, massive armaments, and a shameful inequality in sharing out the goods of the earth. God's gifts are perverted when we misuse them to our own profit or when we try to link them to an ideology, thus forgetting that God is truly creator only when those who receive his gifts are as generous in giving as he is.

Our duty is to rediscover the understanding of our Christian origins, not only those of our two countries but also of the whole of Europe. The same is true of the civilization common to the whole world at the end of the twentieth century insofar as science, technology, and political systems find their origins in Europe. Our world will remain a tragic enigma until it finds itself in the faith which has given it birth. Humanism alone cannot explain us because humanity is not an adequate end for itself; we cannot provide an explanation for ourselves; all we do is isolate ourselves in a closed circle.

The urgent duty of the churches is not first to try to counter as best they can the secularization of institutions. What they must achieve at a deeper level is to enable humankind to rediscover the biblical and Christian bases of modern civilization. Only the faith can allow us to distinguish between good and perverse results of our understanding of the world; only by it can we discern between practices which are inescapably rooted in the faith, even when they try to detach themselves from it.

Thus, for instance, a fanatical nationalism (which is different from a cultural identity which can be legitimate and necessary) is not Christian; but one can understand it as a kind of pagan revival within the religious outlook which has given rise to the modern world, whether it likes it or not. The churches need to bring home to modern countries what they owe to the Bible and to the Gospel. At the heart of Christianity lies toleration. Today, as in the past, the *comprehensiveness* of Anglicanism is a model we can imitate no less than the power of assimilation which is exhibited by Catholicism.

Great Britain's recent history, which has seen the end of the empire, has perhaps shown us the way of dispossession and conversion. Our common task is not only to reestablish communion between churches which are themselves disunited, as Père Congar has rightly said, nor even to bring about a realization of the biblical and Christian foundations of our civilization. These aims will only be achieved if we are personally converted to the values of forgiveness and mercy; they alone can save us by the grace of Christ. Our duty is not simply to show forth these values. We must run the risk of sharing the fate of our crucified Lord by exhibiting them in all their starkness.

We cannot be surprised by the fact that love is not loved. The real question is: What price are we prepared to pay if we are not to disappoint the expectations of humankind now that it can see that humanism cannot save it?

In 1940 your great Prime Minister Winston Churchill had the courage to proclaim at one and the same time the certainty of victory and the sacrifices which it required. In the same way our stern duty is to proclaim to Christians, and to all, the fidelity which is involved by our baptismal state. Doubtless this calls for a courage which is, in the full sense of the word, supernatural. But surely we have received the grace to ask humbly for just that; we must be confident that in the end this grace will be granted.

PEACE AND
RECONCILIATION
*

The Illusions and the Hope

*E*very day the news gives us a picture of a world broken and torn. What is wrong do you think with the people of today?

Ever since humankind has been conscious of its own history, the world has seemed to it to have something wrong with it. We have always had this nostalgia for paradise, for a perfect community involving a sharing of being for the whole of humanity. Some people see this as mere illusion about a past which never existed; others see it as a dream for the future of humanity. For Christians it is vitally important to be able to understand and to explain what the significance is of this broken state and this nostalgia for unity which every person carried within himself or herself. From being an illusion and a dream, they must become a hope. That is our belief.

When you spoke to the Katholikentag at Düsseldorf last summer, you said how worried you were by the events in Lebanon; this was at a time when acts of terrorism were on the increase. Don't you think that our world sees more violence than in the past?

Our world is subject to terrible threats. They appear to us all the more threatening for belonging to the historical situation we are in. It is *our* problem *today*. But if one wants to understand what we are experiencing today, one must understand why the history of humankind has always been a history of broken hopes.

Don't some of the violent events of today seem to you to be more serious than others?

Would they be worse than what went on in the ancient world between slaves and free men, or between Rome and Byzantium? I just don't know. What about the total ignorance which separated human groupings in Africa, Asia, or America? Before the great geographical discoveries, humankind was composed of lost brothers and sisters. Were not these divisions greater than

An interview with Jean-Claude Petit and Michael Cool, in *La Vie*, 31 March 1983.

today? If you analyze today's situation only in terms of today's politics, which is what everybody does, including the papers, then you cannot realize the scale of the divisions which have occurred in the history of humankind.

What Christians have to do by the light of faith is to help humankind to discover and understand what really is at stake. Christians will thus be making an original contribution. Thus, if one is always saying that the only problem today is the economic conflict between north and south and the ideological conflict between East and West, then one forgets a major aspect of history, namely, that it has always been a field of battle for the conflicts which inhabit the human heart, whether in the East, the West, the north, or the south. So the conflict which is part of the human condition can help us to understand the conflicts which we experience today.

Does this mean that you are not worried by the possibility of war?

I want to answer your question without yielding to the imagination of terror. There are real and serious risks of war. We can tell objectively how serious they are by the stockpiling of weapons, their sophisticated technology, and the multiplication of tension. But no rational explanation, and therefore no accurate forecast, has yet been given for these conflicts. So one can only surmise whether a conflict is near or far on the basis of feelings or irrationality. Getting people to panic does not seem to me a responsible way of talking about these problems.

Do you mean that it could be harmful rather than helpful for people to band together to try and ward off these risks or to hide them?

What I am trying to say is that when we are analyzing a real situation, what we should perhaps be doing is having a further look at the underlying tensions and causes of division. It is better if we want to understand what is at stake to start from a Christian interpretation of history rather than from panic or the contradictions which dominate public opinion. In fact the manipulation of public opinion is a part of the strategy of the great powers in their conflict. Fighting for peace does not mean making people afraid of the Russians to help the Americans or vice versa. Our task as Christians is to offer a new way of understanding the history of humankind.

How then can Christians today work for reconciliation between people?

If you use the word *reconciliation* you could be promoting the illusion that a little goodwill is enough to solve all the problems. This can uphold the utopia that we can have peace cheaply, without facing the opposition to it or the real nature of the ills we are facing. This leads to bitter disappointment, cynicism, to complete indifference, to selfish isolationism, and thus to making the antagonisms worse. If people are disillusioned, they will say: "I won't be had again. Each one for herself and the devil take the rest."

So this illusory kind of reconciliation has no contact with reality and no program; it cannot galvanize the great mass of humanity into action. It is dangerous because it could discredit, even in the eyes of Christians, hope in the reconciliation accomplished by Christ and in the active power of God's mercy to solve the conflicts brought about by hatred.

What is true reconciliation then?

Here is what Paul says about it in his letter to the Corinthians: "All this is from God who through Christ reconciled us to himself and gave us the ministry of reconciliation; that is, God was in Christ reconciling the world to himself, not counting their trespasses against them, and entrusting to us the message of reconciliation. So we are ambassadors for Christ, God making his appeal through us. We beseech you on behalf of Christ, be reconciled to God" (2 Cor. 5:18–20).

For Christians reconciliation is not an easy formula for healing the tensions and divisions of the world. Reconciliation has to be accepted as a grace from God. It is the grace of a personal conversion which frees us from sin and from the fundamental break with God. It is through Christ that God accomplishes this liberation of the world. Christians can only become ministers of reconciliation by sharing in Christ's own work, the work of redemption. True reconciliation is the mystery of the cross and the victory of Christ over death. So, when Christians talk of reconciliation, they are talking about the power of the mystery of Christ at work in this world and in the depths of the human heart. Only the action of God, reconciling us with himself by Christ, can change the human heart. Only God can forgive, that is, restore life and give back to the guilty the wholeness of their innocence. Only God can reconcile because he is the creator. The inescapable result of divisions is death, and human creatures alone cannot conquer death. How can one reconcile to each other those who died in the First World War? How can one reconcile the corpses on the battlefields? How can you reconcile to their torturers the victims of the concentration camp and gas chamber?

What is at stake in fact when we talk about reconciliation? To put everything right in the world, is it enough to make a few concessions and to be nice to one another? Are we talking about a universal "settlement out of court"? In that case, would all the victims and the crimes count as profit or loss? Can you envisage the work of reconciliation in the real sense of the word without a sharing in the work of Christ in all its depth? Think of Dag Hammarskjöld, secretary general of the United Nations. His mission led him to undertake the patient work of trying to solve conflicts by mediation, the very thing that I am rejecting as being an insufficient way of looking at reconciliation. But Dag Hammarskjöld himself understood that the mystery of being a Christian is much deeper than the task of a negotiator; he accepted this mystery, even at the cost of his life. So when Christians talk about reconciliation, they are not limiting their view to that of the skillful intermediary between opponents, useful and necessary though such a task may be.

If Christians take the words of the Second Letter to the Corinthians seriously, the practical task of reconciliation, which they are called to live out, implies their own reconciliation with God, hence their own conversion and the acknowledgment of their sins, their unfaithfulness, and their divisions. This reconciliation with God, which is freely given, reestablishes communion with their brothers and sisters. It allows them to share in the mission which Christ wills to fulfill in them. One way or another, they will therefore have a share in the Passion of Christ, as he himself warned his disciples. When he sends them on a mission, as Paul says, carrying the word of reconciliation, the love of which they are the witnesses consumes them in death and in life.

So what you are saying is that Christians must go back to their origins before they undertake anything?

Ordinary common sense will lead any human being worthy of the name to work ceaselessly for peace and reconciliation. But how can one prevent such vague benevolence from turning to disappointment when it is faced with the bitter fact that evil and violence just will not go away? One must face the problem at a deeper level. The Christian response reaches this level and is thus able to face the violence and the evil which run through human history.

We look to the Church to be a place of reconciliation and a sign of reconciliation, especially during Holy Year and the Synod. Do you think this is the sort of Church we have got?

There is no other Church than the Church we have got. The whole point is that the Church is what it is by the grace of God. There is no alternative Church; there is no Church yet to come. The Church was born from the blood of Christ and it is made up of us, poor sinners. The Church must accept that it comes from the grace of God, but to be a sign it does not have to put itself forward as a sign. When the Church wants to be a sign, it becomes a caricature. It is God who uses the Church as it is, with all its limitations, to make it into a sign. It is a temptation to want to produce a "show Church" and "show conversions," just as it is a temptation to want to reduce politics to a show. If I were to try to define an ideal Church as a sign of reconciliation, I feel this would be unreal and a sort of spiritual lie, both for myself and for other people. One always becomes a sign of God in spite of oneself and without knowing it. God does not need actors or publicity agents to make himself known. What he needs is saints, and he chooses them among the poor and humble. But he does the choosing and they don't know about it.

Talking about reconciliation brings to mind the possible unity of the churches. Do you think that ecumenism has come to a standstill?

No, I don't think so at all. If one says that ecumenism is standing still, then one is interpreting it as the world does. One is reducing it to the level of the OPEC discussions or the Geneva negotiations and waiting for a daily news release.

But ecumenism is really a permanent aspect of the life of the Church. It is God's action in reconciling Christians who are human beings divided by their sins. The historical divisions which led to the separations between Christians can be precisely identified; there have been divisions between the East and the West, Byzantium and the non-Byzantine churches, then Constantinople versus the Latin Church, and then the Reformation. These historical divisions come from sins or the effects of sins which can be historically dated. We still bear the marks of these divisions and we have to work in order to overcome them. They can only be overcome if one goes back to their causes.

If sin be the cause of division, then reconciliation can only be brought about by going to the root of sin. It will not be achieved only by the work of professional negotiators but by the effective bringing together of all those who are the heirs of these historic churches. There have been cases in history of church union negotiated at the highest level, but which later came to nothing. The most famous is the Council of Florence where, under massive political pressure, the reunion of the Eastern Orthodox Church and the Western Church was proclaimed; the alternative was the collapse of the Byzantine Empire. Even today the texts of the Council of Florence remain as a possible basis for the effective union of the Byzantine Church and the Latin Church; they are wonderful texts. From the point of view of negotiations, nothing needs to be added to them. One could quite well say: "OK. Let's start the Council of Florence again." But the trouble was that this sort of method did not go to the root of things. Hardly was the Council of Florence over than it became clear that nothing had happened at a grass-roots level.

I think that the situation is different today because there is a widespread hope of reconciliation and of a return to the communion of all the Christian churches. I would say that could be on the horizon for our generation. It has become a possibility because the members of the churches have been along a path of conversion, as have the leaders of the churches and the churches themselves. It is not just a process of getting used to each other. When Paul VI went to Constantinople and when he went to Jerusalem with Patriarch Athenagoras, they experienced these events as a spiritual journey. If you don't understand that, you don't understand the power which is at work. If church leaders are on their own and if the mass of the faithful don't go along the path with them, there will be no unity. One can see this because of the new divisions which occur as we move forward. New schisms are springing up all the time. This is because the human heart is basically incapable of allowing itself to be grasped by the power of God's love.

The unity of the Church is not something natural which occurs spontaneously. Divisions are there right from the start. The unity established by Christ is the result of the strength of his love which masters the powers of division. It is like a creative act of God by which he brings men and women together in spite of the temptation to division. What ecumenism does is not to wipe out the record of past events in history; it must make this power of Christ present so that we can face up to the faults of the past. What is much more important is that this power of Christ will allow us to face up to future quarrels between brothers and sisters. With it we can overcome the temptation to division and the rejection and the hatred which are a permanent feature of the human heart. The work for unity is for all time; it must always face up to the temptation to division while welcoming as a gift the reconciliation which comes from God.

Reasons for Living and
Reasons for Dying

How can one human being ask another human being to die? How can one have any right over the life of one's brothers or sisters? Can there be reasons for living which are so strong that they are also reasons for dying?

Such a question could appear lacking in respect because the answer is so obvious. Ever since our human species has begun to make its way through the darkness of past ages, there have always been men and women, both young and old, who have been prepared to risk their lives and to sacrifice them in order to save those who are close to them. We have been through conflicts which have claimed so many victims; our survival as a nation has been due to the sacrifice of so many men and women. Our honor and our dignity as free persons have been saved by the generosity and by the heroism of many from those generations which have gone before and which are represented here.

But there can be something ambiguous about reasons for living which are presented as reasons for dying. People are often afraid of being taken in by them. This has frequently been written and said in ways ranging from sarcasm to indignation. Surely the thought must have crossed everyone's mind at one time or another that on the other side of the frontier, as formerly on the other side of the front, there are men and women with feelings much like ours who are also convinced that right and justice are on their side. They too used to think that their reasons for living were good reasons for dying, and therefore that their reasons for dying were good reasons for killing.

Can there ever be sufficient motives according to right reason for dying and killing? Can such self-sacrifice and such destruction of self and of others

A homily preached at the mass commemorating the armistice of 1918 at the Church of Saint Louis des Invalides, Paris, 11 November 1982.

141

ever be required? When Christ was put to death two things were said which are very similar and which supply an answer to my question. These two sayings are linked although they are separated by a great gulf.

The first saying was uttered by the political leaders of the people at the time when they were deliberating in secret on the possibility of putting Jesus to death. "It is expedient that one man should die for the people" (John 2:50). This reasoning is inspired by reasons of state, since they know that this man is innocent. Innocence counts for little in their calculations of what seems to them to be reasonable. But can a nation survive if it flouts the rights on which it is based and which justify its existence? "It is expedient that one man should die for the people." Is it possible for the leaders of a nation to destroy its reasons for living in order to ensure its survival? Note that the writer of the Gospel adds that the one who said this was a prophet without knowing it.

The second saying, spoken by Jesus himself, helps us to understand. "Greater love than this has no man, that a man lay down his life for his friends" (John 15:13), and he also said: "No one takes my life from me for I have power to lay it down and to take it up again" (John 10:18). This time we hear the accents of a generous and total love speaking; this is not love of self, or a love of one's relatives, which would be selfish still, but the love of everyone, including one's enemies. Love finds in itself the inexhaustible fountain of life, which makes it possible to give life, but also makes it possible to give one's own life so that those whom one loves may live.

A strange paradox is called to mind by these two sayings about the life of Jesus. No power in the world, neither the state, nor the nation, nor the ties of blood, nor social belonging, can take the place of the absolute value which underlies them all. The Church itself would cease to exist if it claimed to take the place of its Lord. The tyranny of totalitarianism rears its head the moment any of these powers tries to establish its authority by grasping what is of absolute value and identifying with it. Such a use of power dehumanizes instead of being at the service of human beings in their supreme dignity and allowing their humanity to reveal itself. Instead of fulfilling human beings, as it claims to do, it dispatches them as surely as any executioner. It annihilates at the very moment when it claims to impose on them reasons for living; in fact it sends them to their death. There always remains in every human being the hidden secret of its dignity. The slightest ray from the sun of justice is enough to rouse this secret even when the darkness seems to have swallowed it up. The exact nature of this essential point of reference, by which we know what it is to be a human being, is something that escapes exact definition and must always do so. It must remain ever beyond our grasp, above us so that we can remain upright, dominating us so that we can stay free, giving us our being so that we can exist. I will give it its name since it created humankind in its image and likeness. We call it "Our Father in heaven." He it is whose infinite love is revealed in his Son and in the Spirit which dwells in us. The

Spirit is our hidden guest; he brings all humanity together into one single body and bestows on it the possibility of living according to its true dignity. It is not necessary to know about the Spirit or to give it a name in order to be convinced that the humanity of humankind, that highest and most mysterious quality, the basis of all our rights, derives its invincible power of survival from something beyond itself. The true greatness of humankind lies in the fact that it is beyond the power of human beings.

The reasons for which the state can mobilize the nation are finally greater than the state itself. The justification needed by the nation in order to use all the resources of civil society is something greater than the nation. The reason for which a people must survive and must sometimes run the risk of dying is greater than society itself. The state, the nation, and society must respect and defend this reason above all things; it is the humanity of humankind itself and it belongs to no one. The power of the state is only firmly based when it accepts that it is not its own reason for existence. Only love springing from truth can lead to the free sacrifice of themselves by those who would otherwise be driven to meaningless destruction.

The Church can make mistakes in the way it assesses and judges history; but it does not make a mistake when it witnesses to the absolute value which is present in history. It does not err when it defends that which ensures that the human being is a human being worthy of life and worthy of risking his or her life for the sake of life. In order to accomplish its mission the Church receives an infallible guarantee when, following in the steps of Christ, it witnesses to the absolute love which gives to humankind its being. The Church must give this witness in spite of everything and in doing so it is attesting to a value to which it must be the first to submit. Only absolute love is greater than humankind and from it humankind receives its greatness.

Overcoming Fear

I *want to talk about another side of liberty. The American bishops have a major role in the movement for peace and nuclear disarmament. Why does the Church not play such a part in France?*

First of all, may I say that you obviously do not know about certain statements by French bishops which started a campaign among us, especially against the arms trade.[1] Then I want to say that the statement of the American bishops has to be seen in the context of a change in the defense policy of the United States. One has to take into account the long tradition of isolationism in America. From such a point of view the defense of Europe is the equivalent of the defense of an outpost.

That doesn't seem to do justice to the protest of the American bishops which is mainly a statement about morality.

Their criticism of atomic weapons is based on recent strategic theories. They presuppose the rearmament of nations, investment on a large scale in sophisticated conventional weapons, and, up to a point, a remilitarization of society.

Anyway, what the American bishops have done is to condemn the atomic arms race. But France has the atomic bomb. Do you condemn it?

During the last twenty years the Church has issued several very clear statements on the question. However, I am afraid that public opinion concentrated too easily on "localized conflicts," and tries to give itself a good conscience by refusing atomic weapons in principle. Is it better to die by the sword, gas, the machine gun, or the atomic bomb? Is there a clean way of killing people? All war is horrible. We must find a way to ban war.

However, having said this, I must add that the destructive power of atomic weapons, which have been stockpiled by East and West as a way of solving

An interview with Klaus-Peter Schmid in *Der Spiegel,* 11 January 1983.
1. See *Gagner la paix* (Paris: Centurion, 1983). (Translator's note)

144

conflicts, is such that the very future of our planet is in danger. The cost of such armaments is sheer madness. John Paul II has commissioned a report from the Pontifical Academy of Sciences which has been written by scientists from many countries, including Eastern Europe. This report studied the effects of an atomic war upon the world. It has been sent by the pope to the heads of those states which have atomic weapons. There has been very little publicity about this initiative. Was it reported in *Der Spiegel?*

What about the American bishop who said to workers in an atomic factory: "You guys mustn't work in this factory anymore!" Could that happen in France?

Nothing is impossible. But if one takes up that sort of position, it needs to be thought through and thought over. The time the American bishops took to produce their text shows that the solution is not a straightforward one and that they were far from unanimous.

Sometimes people are surprised at the prudent attitude of the French Church, especially as the relations between Church and state in France are the same as in America. The Church is separate from the state and is thus free to say what it likes. But what is different is that you would immediately have a great conflict with the state if you took up the same position as the American bishops.

What would happen above all would be deep divisions in public opinion which is not at all clear on the question, any more than the experts are. We bishops do not deal with this problem independently of the state of the national conscience on the subject (and I don't just mean public opinion). What is needed is a real public debate which would arouse the responsibility of the whole nation and the sense of national identity. The political majority and the opposition have rather similar positions in this matter. How do you explain this? By the nationalism of the French? Don't forget that in modern times our country has been destroyed and bled white three times in less than a century by major wars which it did not begin.

Really, you do have an extraordinary way of accepting the situation!

Well, you seem to be adopting an oversimple situation which seems surprising to us French. The problem of armaments is a clear example of morals in politics; as such it is a problem for the conscience of the French people. But this is not a reason for rushing to adopt some mythology on the subject. We as bishops would not be helping the conscientious decision of the nation if we were to back up emotional campaigns, especially when it is often not clear what their real motives are. We have no interest in fostering or using panic.

What panic are you talking about?

I mean the fear which leads either to overstocking arms or to disarmament. Our job is not to bay with the pack; we have to awaken consciences, to appeal to the reason of the nation, and to contribute to a real debate on morality which all nations should undertake together.

What Does One Fight For?

Questions of peace and war seem to loom large in the relations between the Church and political powers throughout the world. Can I ask you frankly: Would you go and bless the French missiles on the Albion Plateau?

No, I would not. But I must say that the problems of defense are extremely difficult to master by reason alone. On the basic question, I do not want to enter into the highly technical debate on the use of atomic weapons and on the morality or the nonmorality of the various strategies which are proposed. There are, however, certain principles which remain clear. On one side are the risks we are running: a mad arms race and the risk of blowing up the planet with a war so horrible that one can scarcely imagine it. On the other side is the fact that one must be able to defend oneself, one's rights, and one's freedom. Having established these two starting points, is it only possible to say that one is powerless to do anything? Is it impractical to hope that there can be an international juridical structure which would allow the settlement of conflicts? This may well be a utopia in the short run, but it is the position which the Church stubbornly maintains because it indicates where the salvation and the progress of humanity are to be found in the long run.

As regards French defense policy in its specific and original aspects, I cannot forget in view of my age that our country has been bled white twice in this century. The effects of this on morality, society, and politics have been appalling for the dignity of our nation. I do not think that the problem of peace and war can be reduced to armaments, their nature and their size. It is first of all a problem for the conscience of a nation. Why does one ever pay the ultimate cost of laying down one's life? If a nation wants to survive, it

An interview with Gérard Dupuy and Luc Rosenzweig, in *Libération*, 27 September 1983.

146

must have reasons for living. Just to want to defend one's comfortable standard of living is not enough.

Or else there can be attempts to mobilize a nation by the aggressive slogans of a totalitarian regime that means falling into fanaticism. But real democracy means being able to say: "I am willing to give my life because that is what the defense of my children, of my freedom, and of my neighbor is worth."

The Gift of Mercy

I am speaking to you from Paris. I speak to you without seeing you, as one speaks to someone in the dark. Perhaps will I thus be able to say things to you that I could not say if I were looking you in the eye; perhaps you will be able to take them, whereas if you were looking me in the eye you could not do so.

So now I would like to say to you simple things that have been buried for years in silence, things that are very difficult to hear, as they are very difficult to put into words.

We both know that the fact that I have been invited to this Katholikentag means a lot. I am archbishop of Paris; that represents a great deal of history, much of it painful and tragic, in which you are involved. You have also invited Cardinal Francis Macharski, archbishop of Cracow. Auschwitz is in his diocese. I have said enough for you and me to understand that there are things which are hard to say and which must be said nonetheless.

Perhaps the young people among you do not clearly understand what I am alluding to. Perhaps they think that I am brooding over insubstantial memories. But those of you who are as old as I, or older, understand what you hear. You understand because, in spite of the determination to forget, you are like me; sometimes in spite of ourselves we can't help remembering.

This is what happened to me about twenty years ago in Munich. I have only mentioned it to a few friends in France; it is something personal and insignificant, but I have never been able to talk about it to any of my German friends. At the time I had already been back to Germany fairly often. I had seen postwar Germany, rebuilt after its destruction. I had made many friends in different walks of life and I knew what was going on in those years. I wanted to do what I could to help towards the reconciliation between our two countries. I avoided talking about the war years, the deportations, the

A talk given on Radio-Cologne for the Katholikentag, 29 August 1982.

148

persecutions and the concentration camps because I considered this to be a reasonable, peace-making and Christian way to behave.

At the time I was Student Chaplain. After a gruelling year of ministry, I thought I would go to Munich which I knew already. I had taken part in the World Eucharistic Congress there with much interest and great spiritual joy. At the Congress I had discovered a very attractive side of the Church. I had been welcomed to Munich and had felt at home there. That's why I decided to go off on the spur of the moment to see it again; it was the beginning of August.

I got out of the train and stopped with my suitcase on the square outside Munich Station. The sun was shining brightly; the place radiated happiness. Suddenly things changed before my eyes. Passers-by were coming and going, people of my age and older. Suddenly their faces, their features, appeared to me as they had done twenty years previously during the war. I said to myself in great anguish: these people I am seeing now, where were they, what were they doing then? What did they do and not do? Which of them are innocent and which are the others? I suddenly felt that their enigmatic faces had become like masks before my silent questioning. I couldn't feel anything except great distress and sadness. I couldn't stay in that place; I just couldn't exist there. I came to myself and grabbed my suitcase to go back to Paris at once. There wasn't another train that day. I took a room in a nearby hotel and the next morning I went back.

Can you imagine it? This is the first time that I have mentioned what happened to German people. Isn't it strange. And yet I have always had many friends from Germany, both priests and lay people. Many of them have been and are still real brothers to me. But what I have been saying to you, I have never been able to say to them.

If I have taken you into my confidence today, perhaps it is because we both need to start with a confession. There is a silence which paralyzes us and our two countries; it is the silence of shame and fear. It is an evil silence which prevents life and mercy.

I accepted to come and speak to you at the Katholikentag because I thought that this time it was God who wanted me to come and talk. It seemed an impossible thing to do and it remains so from the point of view of human strength, feelings, and memories; and yet I knew I had to do it because God was asking me to. He was asking me and not someone else, just as he had called me to be one of his priests and archbishop of Paris. I don't know how I shall manage it nor what I shall be given to say, but I know that what I am being asked to do, you are being asked to do as well. If God is asking me to do this, it is not only for myself; it is for you too. God is calling you to give witness as well; not only for me, that is of little importance, but for those I am representing, for my Church, for peace and communion between our two countries. God is doubtless asking you to give me a witness, the witness of what he is achieving in you through his forgiveness, for God loves you. You must witness to what he does for you, a work of mercy, truth, and peace.

Yes, I must talk of forgiveness and of a change of heart. But who is to be forgiven? What sort of forgiveness can man give? Do we who are still alive have the power to blot out what has happened so that it never occurred? No one can obliterate the past. Human reparation is impossible. Even if human laws make us the heirs of those who are dead, one does not inherit from death itself.

At the most, human forgiveness can only be a loss of memory. One behaves as if the acts committed did not take place, as if nothing had occurred. In the end human pardon is a kind of forgetting. Forgetting means contempt because the one who has sinned against God and humanity is left with the burden of fault and in solitude. Those who remember the evil that was done are left with the pain of what cannot be undone.

In fact the best thing one can do is to forget. But if one forgets the executioner, one also forgets the victim, especially if it has died. Even if, before the victim died, it was able to forgive the executioner for the evil which it suffered and even if it washed its heart clean of all hatred, still it cannot deliver the conscience of the executioner from the evil which the executioner has done. By oneself one cannot forgive the sin of another. There lies the depth of evil and its irreparable character. One can give back an object, repair a house, or repay a sum of money. One cannot give back life; one cannot blot out guilt or restore a state of innocence.

Forgiveness is not in our power; only God can forgive.

True forgivenesss cannot be anything else than a resurrection from the dead. Only God can raise up the dead. It is the heavenly Father who gives to us in his only Son, the suffering Messiah, a pledge of this resurrection and its reality. The Crucified One spoke on the cross the words of forgiveness when, as the only Son, he spoke to the Father. He did not say "I forgive you." He said "Father, forgive them for they know not what they do."

Christ as the only begotten, handed over to destruction, implored from the Father the forgiveness which only the Father can give. The proof that this pardon is granted is the Resurrection of the Son. Yet the Risen One still bears the marks of the Passion. The Resurrection does not mean that the Passion is forgotten. The wounds of the risen Son of God are no longer signs of dejection and condemnation for those who caused them, like the soldiers, or those who aided and abetted because they were silent or fled, like the disciples. On the contrary, his wounds are now the sign of healing and salvation. From now on his wounds can be touched and they are offered as a place of grace and a source of certainty when Jesus holds out his hands to Thomas. On the cross already, as John tells us, "one of the soldiers pierced his side with a spear and at once there came out blood and water" (John 19:34).

This is the source of life, of reconciliation and forgiveness, of divine life and of the Spirit given to humankind.

God alone can forgive because God alone can save. God's forgiveness does not obliterate our unhappy history; it redeems it. He gives it back to us in his forgiveness. He makes it possible for us to receive it with a broken heart as a source of redemption and not of condemnation, a place of salvation and not of dereliction. The innocent victim who was pierced is the mediator of the new covenant and its High Priest. When Jesus raises up the paralytic "that you may know that the Son of man has authority on earth to forgive sins" (Matt. 9:6), he shows forth that he can use on earth the Father's power of showing mercy. For only the creator can be the redeemer. It is impossible for us to forgive, but the disciples of Christ receive from the well-beloved Son not only the power to forgive sins in his name but the mission to do so. In his name they can bestow the forgiveness which belongs to the Father in heaven.

I came to this gathering of your Church to recall the words of Jesus whose minister I am. I can say that the God who grants mercy to all grants mercy to you. I come to say the words of forgiveness which are those of the Messiah.

There is one more secret thought I must share with you. Perhaps you will find it consoling and hopeful. Here it is: the suffering of the victims and their death are a part of the suffering of the Messiah. They are gathered into the chalice of God as are the tears of his children; through his Messiah, God makes them become a water of purification. I like to think that in the secret of God, when the innumerable victims who are united to Christ in his Passion receive his forgiveness, they are also united to him in bestowing forgiveness on others.

Finally, as you know, if we are granted mercy, it is so that we in our turn can show mercy to others; each of us received the grace for this and each of us received the calling to be the witnesses of that mercy. I pray to God that you too may be for us and for all the witnesses of forgiveness and its instruments.

I have spoken to you as a brother in Christ. Since I have reached you by my voice only, without our being able to see each other, like travelers in the night, I have spoken to you under the shelter of that night. It is the night of the Passover, night of death and of life, which makes it possible to speak to one another again. May you receive my words as a gift which God has made it possible for me to make to you.

A Trial Indicating the
Spiritual Destiny of Our Times

Is the practice of the sacrament of penance, as we have received it in the tradition of the Church, likely to fall into disuse for an indefinite length of time? This is not a purely theoretical anxiety since the sacraments have their own history, a history which indicates the spiritual progress of Christian peoples.

What has happened in the case of the Eucharist should give food for thought. For many centuries, in the Eastern churches as in the West, *the receiving of Holy Communion by the people became so rare that it nearly disappeared.* This long period when the eucharistic body of Christ was no longer shared in abundance among the baptized was also the time when the ecclesial body of Christ suffered the dramatic divisions which still affect it today. On the other hand, is it not possible that there is a link between the return to frequent communion and the birth of an ardent desire and a firm decision to work for the unity of the ecclesial body of Christ which are revealed in the Catholic Church by the ecumenical movement?

If it is true that there is today the danger that the practice of the sacrament of penance and reconciliation is fading away, especially the personal confession of sins and the personal receiving of forgiveness, then we should see this as being for the Church a trial indicating the spiritual destiny of our times, one of the temptations which the Church carries in its flesh.

A Time of Violence, Doubt, and Mass Movements

We have entered a period of extreme violence which is reaching its climax in the threat of the self-destruction of humanity. Men and women have lost

Contribution to the Synod of Bishops, 4 October 1983, published in *Documentation Catholique*, 6 November 1983.

faith in personal action as being able to avert such collective forces. How brave Christians would have to be to believe in the effectiveness of a personal confession of failure concerning the respect for life that God requires of them!

We have entered a period when human reason has tried to set up conflict as a scientific law of progress in history. Men and women are dubious about the effectiveness of a personal love which shows mercy. How brave Christians would have to be to believe in the effectiveness of a forgiveness which is received and shared and which gives the strength to love one's enemies as children of the same Father in heaven!

We have entered a period of mass movements where everyone feels powerless to change a collective destiny and thus loses a sense of responsibility. Men and women are dubious about the effect on humanity of the offering up of their liberty in secret. What courage Christians are going to need to receive from Christ the penance and the compassion of a contrite heart which unites them to the task of saving the world!

We have entered a time of collective guilt; men and women do not see that a personal word of repentance can have any significance. What courage Christians are going to need in order to receive from Christ the savior the hope of pardon and the joy of deliverance where the Spirit anticipates the Resurrection!

The Testing of the Church and of the World

The Church in its sacramental practice is being tested in the same way as the world is being tested in its dignity and its aspirations. The Second Vatican Council wanted to renew the sacrament of penance, as received from the tradition expressed at the Council of Trent. The fact that this renewal does not seem to have had all the results expected is not unconnected with the historical situation of our times. Similarly there are doubtless good reasons why we are being tested in connection with this particular sacrament which calls for the decisive exercise of personal responsibility on the part of the baptized sinner.

For the same sort of reasons the world experiences an anonymous fear of destruction and a general but elusive feeling of collective guilt.

In a written note conveyed to the secretariat of the Synod, I have offered some thoughts on the real link between two aspects which are disassociated by the crisis of our times:

1. what the world expects from the Church: an attitude of penance for the mistakes and the faults of the past, a social commitment for justice and peace, and therefore a commitment to work for the reconciliation of humankind;

2. the grace of the sacrament of penance, received individually by each Christian who is sorry for sins and is prepared to confess them humbly as his or her own and to receive forgiveness.

The historical circumstances of the end of the twentieth century require from us a decision which needs a lot of courage: we must not allow the centuries-old tradition of the sacrament of penance to die out. The Church of today has received this tradition; what we must do is show people what riches of church life are contained in this tradition and what personal renewal it implies. If this happens, Christians will become aware that by the sacrament of penance they are constantly being reconciled with God, with their brothers and sisters, and with themselves. They will experience the liberty of sons and daughters of God. They will work tirelessly in the strength of the Holy Spirit to share the reconciliation which they receive from their Father in heaven.

If this happens the Church will be allowing the good things which the Lord has entrusted to it to bear fruit. Thus will the men and women of our time be enabled to discover the one thing that is necessary: light, hope, and love.